LOVING GOD, BUT STILL LOVING YOU

LOVING GOD
BUT STILL
Loving You

Marion Stroud

AMERSHAM-ON-THE-HILL, BUCKS HP6 6JQ
ENGLAND

Conception, Design and Production
Copyright © Nuprint Ltd/Gazelle Books 1995
Harpenden, Herts AL5 4SE

Editorial work by
AD Publishing Services Ltd
Leighton Buzzard, Beds LU7 0SP
England

ISBN 1 898938 18 0

Scripture quotations are taken from:
Good News Bible © *American Bible Society* 1992
New International Version © 1973, 1978, 1984 *International Bible Society*
Living Bible © 1971 Tyndale House

Acknowledgements:
The diagram from *Children Finding Faith* by F. Bridger is used by permission
of Scripture Union; the song 'Wait for Me' by permission of Gay Hyde; and
the illustration from the *Good News Bible* © American Bible Society 1992 used
by permission. We have made every effort to trace copyright holders; our
apologies to any of those we have inadvertently omitted.

British Library Cataloguing in Publication Data.
A catalogue record for this book is available from the British Library.

Designed and Produced in England for
ALPHA PUBLICATIONS
an imprint of Scripture Press Foundation (UK) Ltd
Raans Road, Amersham-on-the-Hill, Bucks HP6 6JQ by
Nuprint Ltd, Station Road, Harpenden, Herts AL5 4SE

This book is dedicated to all those who have shared their joys and their struggles with me, and still live daily with the pain and the potential involved in loving God, and loving the partner who does not yet share their faith.

Contents

Foreword

Every now and again a Christian book is produced that really gets to the heart of the matter. A topic of widespread relevance and concern is matched by an author who is abundantly qualified to write about it. The result is a book of both quality and impact.

Loving God But Still Loving You is one such book. It offers sensitive and constructive advice to Christians whose partners do not share their faith. Marion Stroud, renowned speaker and writer on relationship issues, is unequivocally qualified to write on the subject.

As editor of a women's Christian magazine, I am well aware that the dilemmas facing those married to husbands who are not of their faith are very real to many Christian women today. From my daily postbag and through conversations at Christian women's groups, I have discovered that the subject is indeed a 'hot potato'. But with 90% of the population still not classified as 'regular church-goers' this should come as no surprise.

This book is a timely response. Its strength — and why I believe it has already sold over 70,000 copies in its first edition — is its ability to provide practical answers to the issues facing 'lone' Christian partners. It's a 'how to' book: how to keep your faith, and your marriage, together.

Marion Stroud successfully accomplishes this by

being totally thorough in her approach. Using both professional research and personal case studies, she comprehensively deals with the emotional and circumstantial difficulties that face 'lone' Christians.

Loving God But Still Loving You leaves the reader with a renewed outlook on what is so often seen as a hopeless situation. I believe Marion's book will be of great help to many of us, and I warmly commend it to Christians and to those who are not Christians.

Liz Proctor, *Woman Alive Magazine.*

Introduction

They sat in my lounge drinking coffee, as they had done on so many similar occasions in the past two years. Most of them were young mums like myself, enjoying an opportunity to relax and chat together, and to listen to someone talk about something of general interest, other than toddler tantrums and potty training!

But today there was a difference. Today, our speaker had talked of the effect on her marriage and family when she had come to a personal faith in Jesus, eight years after she married. Usually we discussed what had been said with those sitting nearest, rather than making public comments, but today even the shyest members of the group were provoked into bombarding Maureen with questions.

'What did you say to the children when you believed one thing and your husband believed another?'

'How did you break the news to him that you wanted to go to church?'

'What did you do about the collection in the service? My husband would go mad if he thought that I was giving money to the church. He says that all the clergy are interested in is getting their hands on your wallet.'

'Has it *really* helped your marriage? I'd love to have a faith like yours, but I'm afraid to risk it.'

'I believe in Jesus and my husband doesn't, and it can be awfully lonely sometimes. Couples who come to church together just don't seem to understand.'

This last comment came from Judy, who must have

felt very strongly about the matter, since she'd never opened her mouth in public before!

All that happened over twenty years ago, and in the intervening years, Judy's husband has discovered the reality of God's love for himself. These days they worship together and take an active part in the work of their local church. But there are still many other 'Judy's', and not a few 'Peters', who have either been drawn to the Christian faith after they were married, or found that an earlier commitment has been rekindled. Now they all long to share this most important part of their lives with the people they love best — their marriage partner and their children.

Perhaps you're one of them. You may have been walking with God for many years, or you could have just discovered what it means to have a faith that is real and life-changing. It's possible that you have asked the very questions raised by my friends, and many more beside. On the other hand, you may not yet have made that commitment to Christ, but you're wondering, 'Could it work for me? Is it worth the risk? Dare I take that step of faith?'

Whether you belong to any of those groups of people, or are simply looking for information and insights that will enable you to understand and support a friend in that situation better, this book is for you. Since women appear to come to faith as adults rather more easily than men, there seem to be many more 'Judy's' than 'Peters' around. For that reason I have looked at the subject mainly from the viewpoint of a woman with a 'not-yet-believing' husband, while trying not to ignore the situations where a different approach might be helpful if the man is the believing partner.

You might describe this book as 'faction!'. The Christian teaching to which I refer is all to be found in the Bible, so you can check out the references, and weigh the evidence for yourself. The experiences that people have shared with me are also true, but in order to protect the privacy of the individuals concerned, some stories have been combined, and names and details of the circumstances have been changed.

Some of my friends who have contributed to this book have had difficult and painful situations to deal with. In spite of that, all of them have found that their faith has brought great joy into their lives, which problems might dampen but cannot destroy. None of them have suggested that they would like to turn the clock back to the days before God was a living reality to them. All of them long for the day when they will be able to say with the Psalmist, 'Glorify the Lord with me'…and those whom they love so much will respond, 'Let us exalt His name together.'

'My husband would go mad if he thought that I was giving money to the church. He says that all clergy are interested in is getting their hands on your wallet.'

If there was a fail-safe method of making this happen, I would be delighted to share it with you. Unfortunately life — and people — are not that simple. We have all been given the freedom to choose, and those of us who have chosen to accept God's way of love and forgiveness also have the responsibility of sharing the good news of what we have found to be true with others. Jesus certainly told us to do that. But we need to do it humbly, like one beggar telling another beggar where to find bread — and then leaving him or her to find it. Force-feeding always causes resentment!

And that is only part of our journey. Each of us has to take our own steps along the path from brokenness to wholeness in Jesus. That is our prime responsibility, no matter whom our travelling companions are. For it's when we love and serve Jesus consistently ourselves and allow Him to change us, that we can most effectively become channels of His love and peace to others. If this book helps you to do this, then it will have achieved its purpose.

1

'Help! My Wife's Got Religion'

THREE COUPLES...THREE DIFFERENT SITUATIONS

When one partner in a marriage relationship becomes a Christian or rediscovers their faith, life is never quite the same again for either half of the couple. The newly discovered commitment, joy and sense of purpose that the Christian experiences, are like pebbles that are tossed into the waters of their life together and the ripples spread far and wide. Every part of their relationship and lifestyle are eventually touched. Each situation is unique and special, but here are the stories of three ordinary couples who have experienced God at work in their lives.

Colin and Chrissie: 'I thought that she'd gone barmy'

Colin's hands clenched involuntarily as he thought back to the way he'd felt when his wife stopped merely taking their children to Sunday School at the Baptist church, and stayed for the service herself. 'My Mum and Dad had never gone to church, and they hadn't sent me to Sunday School. All I knew about the Bible and Christianity, were RE lessons at school and Parade services in the Navy, and I'd have applied the same word to both — *boring!* I just couldn't see why Chrissie felt a need for it. I'd got a reasonable sort of job. We had a house, and two lovely kids — why would she want to go to church, for goodness' sake?'

At the time Chrissie would have been hard pressed to answer that question. Her childhood experiences of faith had certainly been different. She had enjoyed Sunday School in the village church and Scripture lessons in the stone-built school that nestled beside it. They had been one of the more pleasurable parts of being evacuated from wartime London to the comparative safety of the country. But when she returned to 'normal life', God was no longer part of her teenage thinking — until she had her own children.

'When I had Hilary I felt quite scared,' she said. 'Bringing up a baby seemed to be such a responsibility. We'd just moved, and my Mum lived miles away. So when the Health Visitor suggested that I might like to go to the mid-week Pram Service at the church down the road, I thought "Why not?" At least it would get me out of the house, and give me the chance to make some new friends. As they got older the children tended to move on to Sunday School as a natural thing and so I'd take Hilary and Patrick down to the church on a Sunday morning and leave them with their teacher, while I cooked the dinner and Colin cleaned the car.'

This state of affairs might have continued, if Wendy, one of her neighbours, hadn't invited Chrissie to a coffee morning. 'Please say you'll come,' Wendy urged. 'We've got this missionary nurse staying, and I said that I'd have a meeting at my house so that people could hear about her work in the refugee camp...and we could raise a bit of money...you know the sort of thing. But lots of my neighbours can't come, and it will be so embarrassing if there are only two or three people there!'

More to help her friend than out of any great interest, Chrissie agreed to go — and found the morning to be a revelation!

'I'd never met anyone like her before,' she said. 'Here was someone of about my own age, who seemed to have a hot line to heaven! God was her friend. She said that He spoke to her, and told her what to do when she had a problem. She pointed out that there was a vast difference between knowing *about* God, and knowing Him for ourselves. She talked about being forgiven and having a completely new start in life...like being born all over again. I don't remember them ever mentioning that at the Pram Service!

'Anyway, when she prayed a prayer at the end of her talk, and said that anyone who wanted to make this "fresh start" could pray it with her, I did, although I hadn't understood everything she'd said. I just knew that if God really could be a loving father — something that I had never known but always longed for — rather than a vague "idea" in the background, then that was what I wanted.

'When I talked to her afterwards, she said that there was so much more to being a Christian than praying that prayer, and suggested that I went to church and stayed *with* the children rather than simply taking them. That was the beginning of the change in me and in our marriage, and it's been the most wonderful *and* the most difficult time of my life.'

Meg and James: I'll 'altar' him!

When Colin and Chrissie got married the 'faith factor' was not an issue for them. Colin had never given God a second thought, and Chrissie's vague belief in the existence of God had no impact on her day to day life. For Meg it was very different. She had come to a personal faith in her teens, and embarked on her medical training because she was already considering becoming a missionary doctor. Then a fellow student committed suicide, and Meg was devastated.

'I'd prayed and prayed for John to be healed of his depression,' she said, 'and when he took his own life, I felt as if God had let me down. All the questions about death and suffering that I'd only dealt with on an academic level so far, swept over me, and although I didn't get as far as denying my faith, I made a conscious decision to put it on the back burner.

'Very soon afterwards I went on a sailing holiday, and was flattered when one of the instructors gave me far more attention than my inability to keep the boat on course warranted! James was a "free spirit", unconventional and quite different from the rather serious young men that I'd known in the hospital Christian Union, and I needed to know that *someone* loved me. I told him that I was a Christian, and for a time he seemed quite interested, so that it was very easy to persuade myself that it was only a matter of time before he would come to believe as I did.

'We didn't actually see that much of one another during our courtship because James was working on the sail boats in Greece, and I was studying for exams. So most of our "going out" was done by letter, phone, and the odd snatched weekend. My friends warned me that I was playing with fire by getting emotionally involved with someone whose outlook on life was so different, but I was determined to get married, and this looked like the best opportunity I'd have.

'Little by little I withdrew from my circle of Christian

Opposite directions can wreck a relationship.

friends, and church-going, difficult enough for a hospital doctor, became even more spasmodic than usual. James and our future together was the total focus of my life, and, unbelievable as it seems now, I just never considered how our lifestyles and goals for the future might clash. We'd been married for two months when it finally dawned on me that faith was not the only thing in our lives that we were approaching from an entirely different standpoint.

'The first two years of our marriage were stormy. James was trying to establish his own sailing school, and I was working for further qualifications. I had to take jobs wherever they became available, which meant that I was often away from home, and a tiny flat over a boat chandlers wasn't a very appealing place to come back to. Then it looked as if James was on the verge of bankruptcy, when some huge loans that he had taken on, were called in.

In sheer desperation, I went into the first church I could find that was open, and wept. I recognized that a lot of the problems in my life were of my own making, and I told God how sorry I was for turning my back on Him. I hardly dared to believe that He would listen or forgive me, but as I knelt there, a shaft of sunlight came through the stained glass window and fell across my shoulders. It felt just as if someone had thrown a warm blanket over me, and wrapped me round with acceptance and unconditional love. I *knew* from then on that I'd been absolutely forgiven, but I still had to live with the consequences of my actions, and that is something I've been doing ever since.'

Gina and Roger: Together...Apart

A couple launching out into marriage with no conscious awareness of God in their lives, and a partnership where one of the couple does have a personal faith, however tenuous it may be at the time, are not the only possible scenarios where conflict over the spiritual dimension of life may develop later on. Take Gina and Roger for example. They met when Gina was asked to help Roger lead the church youth club.

'I was fairly new to the area,' said Gina, 'and didn't know many people at the church. But I'd noticed Roger because he was one of those people who was always involved with things. He was very popular, and I felt really excited when he asked me if I would do a skin care and make-up demonstration for the girls in the youth club. After that session, I offered to help with the basketball team, and our romance just blossomed from there. We went to church and Bible studies together and talked for hours about what God might be calling us to do for Him in the future. I had wonderful rosy dreams of being the wife of a minister, or even a missionary, and for the first year or two of our marriage that really seemed likely.

'Then it all went horribly wrong. It started when there were financial problems at the church, and our minister, whom Roger admired very much, left. That really shook his faith. Then work got very demanding, and he often had to do overtime or go on weekend courses, which meant that he missed church. The final straw was when he was asked to give a short talk about how God can be relevant to a businessman's life. He told me afterwards that as he stood at the front of the church he suddenly thought, "I don't think God is relevant in my business life" and that was that. He got through his talk somehow, but he stopped going to church for ten long years, and I felt as if my heart was broken.'

Chrissie, Meg and Gina — three women who all had a very important part of their lives which they couldn't share with their husbands. Thankfully, Gina's situation doesn't occur very often, although it does happen, and so we will look at the implications of that, for the people concerned, a little later on. But far more common is the situation where faith is discovered or rediscovered when a marriage is well under way. What will all this mean in practical terms for the one who's joyfully embracing a new life and a whole new lifestyle? And what about the partner who may be looking on with reactions which could range from pleasure and admiration — as long as it doesn't involve him — to sheer unmitigated horror? How can the new or renewed Christian begin to share the good news with the person who, up till now, has been at the centre of her world?

2

New Life: New Lifestyle?

GROWING, CHANGING, SHARING OUR FAITH

Most of us love the idea of a fresh start. When I was at school, being issued with a new 'rough' book was a special event. Never again, I would tell myself, would the book that I was given for rough notes become messy, decorated with ink splodges or rude messages to my friends. This time I would keep it tidy. Of course, this resolution only lasted for a week or two, rather like the ones I made for the New Year or on my birthday.

Spiritually alive

Some people worry in case their new-found faith turns out to be little more effective than a new year's resolution. But there's a crucial difference between 'turning over a new leaf' and turning our lives over to God. When we come to Him, confessing our disobedience and total inability to live His way, believing that Jesus has taken the punishment that we deserve, and asking for His forgiveness, God does a miracle. We don't just have physical life, but we come alive spiritually as well. The Bible puts it like this:

> **When someone becomes a Christian he becomes a**

> brand new person inside. He is not the same any
> more. A new life has begun.   *2 Corinthians 5:17*, TLB

Now this is a statement of fact, and is true, whether we *feel* it or not. People's emotional reactions to committing their life to God vary enormously. Some folk really do feel 'new all over' and know immediately and without a doubt that their life has taken a completely new direction. Others feel little or nothing at first, and if they rely on how they *feel* might easily wonder if anything has happened to them at all.

For this very reason, feelings cannot be the foundation of our faith. The way we feel can be influenced by the weather, the behaviour of our nearest and dearest and the state of our health or our hormones — to mention just a few factors! So, basing our beliefs on the way we feel can be very misleading. But if this is so, what can we rely on when things around us (including perhaps friends and family) seem to suggest that this new-found faith is merely a figment of our imagination?

Faith is the key word here. C.S. Lewis, who struggled with many doubts before he became one of the greatest champions of Christianity, said, 'Faith is the art of holding firmly to things your reason once accepted, in spite of your changing moods.' Faith assures us that we can rely on God, and on what He says about Himself in the Bible: unlike our feelings, this does not change. The Bible contains so many promises that we can fling at the demons of doubt, and even if we are not very good shots in the normal way, these missiles always home in on their target. Here are some of them:

> For God loved the world so much that He gave His
> only Son, so that everyone who believes in Him
> may not die, but have eternal life.   *John 3:16*, GNB

'Listen! I stand at the door and knock; if anyone hears my voice and opens the door, I will come into his house and eat with him, and he will eat with me.'

Revelation 3:20, GNB

God loves us: if we have believed and committed ourselves to Jesus then we have His unchanging assurance that we are part of His family. What is more, we have His gift of eternal life, beginning right now.

Many people have difficulty in believing that the slate of the past is really wiped clean. God's enemy, Satan, loves to remind us of our faults and failings. But over and over again the Bible reassures us that God has forgiven our wrongdoing in attitude and action. Here are some words from the Old Testament:

The Lord is merciful and loving…He does not keep on rebuking: He is not angry for ever. He does not punish us as we deserve or repay us for our sins and wrongs…. As far as the east is from the west, so far does he remove our sins from us.

Psalm 103:8,9,10,12, GNB

So, with the mistakes of the past put that far away from us, we can enjoy the company of Jesus Christ, day by day, no matter how humdrum or ordinary those days may seem. We may not see Him or hear Him speaking audibly, but we have His promise:

'Be sure of this— that I am with you always, even to the end of the world.' *Matthew 28:20*, TLB

But what about the 'feel good factor'?

'God has said it: I've believed it: that settles it.' This statement, helpful though it is, does give the whole matter of faith a rather clinical feel, doesn't it? But saying that we should take God at His word doesn't mean that He doesn't care about the way we feel. Indeed, He's given us our emotions, and He wants us to experience His love and friendship. This is why Jesus promised that those who believe in Him would be given His Holy Spirit to live within their very personality. In his letter to the Christians at Rome Paul explains:

> **God's Spirit joins Himself to our spirits, to declare that we are God's children.**   *Romans 8:16*, GNB

And when he was writing to the churches in Galatia, Paul pointed out something else. Not only does the Holy Spirit reassure us that we are part of the Christian family, but He also changes us. When the Holy Spirit controls our life He will produce qualities of character which we may naturally lack. He helps us to be more loving, joyful, peaceful, patient, kind and good; faithful, gentle and self-controlled — these are all very much rooted in emotion and feeling.

So we can see that we need both God's Word (the Bible) and His Spirit to strengthen us, and to give us a firm foundation for our belief. Then we can set out confidently on this life of faith and adventure. For let's make no mistake, becoming a Christian or renewing our faith is no soft option. We'll certainly experience the joy of God's love and forgiveness; we may well sense a new purpose and direction in our lives; but because 'no man [or woman] is an island' the choices we make, and the changes that these choices bring into our lives will have an impact on other people, especially the people we love best — our family.

What shall I tell him?

The way in which people come to understand and accept the Christian faith for themselves varies enormously, and so does the way that they share it with others. For some it is a quiet realization that God is real and at work in His world. They have seen Him active in the lives of others, and then the light dawns — this spiritual dimension of life is available for them to enjoy, too! One woman, Anne, described it as the sense of coming into harbour after months on a lone voyage in a stormy sea. Initially, the impact that her discovery had on her homelife was equally gentle.

'I said very little to John about it for a long time,' she said. 'We don't talk much about how we feel, John especially. I'd been going to a series of Lent talks at our church, and so it seemed a natural thing to go to the service on Easter Day. In fact he came with me. After that, going to church on Sunday became part of my weekend routine. I tried to fit in with John's plans, and that wasn't difficult usually. There were several services to choose from, so if I couldn't get to my usual one, I simply went to another.'

Others reach out to God in the midst of a crisis, as Lorna did. Her sister Lizzie, a committed Christian, was killed by teenage joy-riders in a stolen car. When Lorna saw how her brother-in-law and his friends from church dealt with their pain and their questioning, she was determined to find out why they were able to cope with their grief without bitterness.

'I started going to church myself, and one night I had a long talk to the vicar after the service. He said that God understood how I felt, because His Son had been murdered too. But His death had something to do with me. Although I may not have killed anyone, I'd chosen to live my life without reference to God, and I needed forgiving for that. It was actually as a result of Jesus' seemingly pointless death, that I could both be forgiven, and be helped to forgive those kids who killed Lizzie.

'I suddenly felt as if a huge weight had been lifted off my shoulders. I was so excited that I ran home from church with a grin from ear to ear,' she said. 'I blurted it all out to Terry and, to be fair to him, he did listen. Then he patted my shoulder and said that when I'd got over Lizzie's death, I'd probably see things differently. But if it helped me at the moment, it was better than me going on the gin!'

During the next year, Lorna began to come to terms with the loss of her sister, but far from fading away, her faith became more and more important to her. 'Terry was tolerant at first,' she said. 'Although he thinks that any kind of religious belief is an emotional crutch, he could accept that I needed something to help me for a while.

'However, as time has passed and I've wanted to get more involved in the church, he is far from happy. In his view, anyone who admits to being in need, or has to ask for help, is weak and despicable. He thinks that what he calls "the whole Christian myth" is a load of rubbish, and that I'm an idiot for being "taken in" by it. I've tried every argument in the book, but I can't make him see it any differently. I'd like to be confirmed, but when I mentioned it we had such a row that I've had to shelve that idea for the present.'

It is desperately disappointing when those we love either cannot or will not see what appears to be so obvious to us. But don't be too discouraged. The Bible tells us that people who are not yet Christians are blind to the truth about God, until God Himself opens their eyes. Remember, too, that a sense of need is almost always present before we can accept what God has to offer, and the journey to the point of admitting that need is often long and slow.

So what is the situation behind your front door?

Perhaps your nearest and dearest are of the opinion that 'a little bit of religion is fine for Mum if it keeps her happy' but don't want to know for themselves. Maybe they're downright sceptical about the very existence of God, and would label themselves 'Humanist', 'Agnostic', 'Atheist', or plain 'Not Interested'. Whatever our situation, we have certain responsibilities to ourselves and others, as we set out or continue on our journey into wholeness in Jesus. The most basic can be summed up in three simple phrases. We need to consider how to ensure that we're:

- Growing in our faith
- Changed by our faith
- Sharing our faith

Growing in our faith

The Bible speaks of someone who has come to a personal faith as having been 'born again'. The spiritual part of us which was dormant has now sprung into life. But just as a newborn baby has a lot of growing to do before it reaches maturity, so does a spiritual baby. For that to happen we need the right sort of food, fresh air and exercise.

When I was a small child in Sunday School, one of the songs we sang with great gusto (possibly because it involved flinging your arms wide and thumping your neighbour!) had a line in it which said, 'Read your Bible and pray every day if you want to grow.'

Today many of us have lost the reading habit, but if we're going to grow and become strong as Christians, we'll need to make use of the spiritual food that God has provided in the Bible. Some people assume that reading the Bible involves starting at Genesis and plodding through to Revelation, but that is rather like giving

a baby steak and chips, before it has any teeth.
Choking is likely to result!

The Bible isn't just one book, but a whole library
within one set of covers. If you haven't opened it since
school days, the Gospels, in which we see Jesus in
action, are a good place to start. You might compare
these chapters with spiritual milk — easier to digest,
and very suitable for spiritual babies. Let's look at how
three different people approached Bible reading.

---

*Whatever our situation,
we have certain responsibilities
to ourselves and others,
as we set out or continue on our journey
into wholeness in Jesus.*

Lorna. When Lorna came to faith she read the New
Testament through in a fortnight. 'I was so excited
about God,' she said, 'that I just gobbled up everything
I could find out about Him. Then I realized that I had
some idea of the big picture, but it was all too much to
take in at once and now I needed to look at the detail.
On the bookstall at church we had some little cards
with a series of questions on. I started reading through
the Gospel of John, a few verses at a time, used the
questions to help me to think about what I'd read, and
wrote the answers down in a notebook.'

The questions that Lorna used were:

- Do I understand what this passage is about as a
  whole? (If the answer was 'not really' she tried
  reading the same verses in a different version of
  the Bible.)

- What does this passage teach me about God the Father, the Son or the Holy Spirit?
- What does it teach me about life? Is there a warning, a good example, a promise, or a command for me to obey?
- Is there a verse or part of a verse which has something to say to me, that I can remember and think about during the day?

'I didn't always feel as if God spoke to me directly,' she said, 'although quite often He did. For instance when I read about Jesus getting up very early to pray, I realized that this could be the answer for me too. So I prayed straight away for help to get up before the family were astir — I couldn't set my alarm because it would annoy Terry. And I found myself waking up half an hour earlier, all through that summer.'

If you feel that you'd appreciate suggestions about how much to read, and notes to help you understand the more difficult ideas, there are many Bible reading schemes, carefully written to meet the needs of different kinds of people. A modern translation, like the New International Version or the Good News Bible, makes it easier to grasp what God has to say.

Having heard from God, we'll also want to talk to Him in prayer, which one poet described as the 'fresh air for the soul.' Sometimes it's very hard to find the space and quietness in our busy lives to set time aside for God, especially if the rest of the family are unsympathetic.

Anne. Anne's husband didn't mind her going to church, but the sight of her reading the Bible really offended him. So, during the week Anne took her Bible to work with her, and slipped into the nearby Library during her lunch hour. It was quiet, warm and everyone else was reading, so she could spend time with God without causing friction at home.

Sally. Sally had four pre-school children, and her days began very early and ended late. There was usually one precious 15-minute period of quietness at lunchtime when the three older children were watching television and the baby was asleep. But that seemed to be too short to be of any use. Then one day she sensed that God was saying to her, 'Tune in to Me during the morning as you do your chores. See Me in creation as you walk down to playgroup; talk to Me about your family as you iron their clothes, or sing along to a worship tape as you prepare the lunch. Then your heart will be ready to focus on Me, and your ears will be open to hear from Me during your brief moments of quiet.' Somewhat sceptically she tried it, and found that it made a tremendous difference. Instead of being confined to a daily or weekly slot, God became part of the fabric of her very existence.

Changed by our faith

Growth and change are two sides of the same coin. You only have to look at the vast changes that take place as a baby grows from infancy to adulthood to appreciate that. So, as we begin to grow and develop spiritually, we also begin to change. We've already seen that the Holy Spirit gradually produces new qualities of character within us — sometimes, it seems, painfully slowly. As we change inwardly, we'll begin to act and react differently as well, and it's this which will have the greatest impact on those around us.

Some people find it easy to explain things. Others prefer to 'show' rather than to 'tell'. And however much they may talk about it, most people seem to find that deeds not words are the things that count most in convincing others that something real has taken place. This was the experience of Jenny and Paul.

When Jenny greeted Paul on the doorstep with the information that she had been 'born again' that very afternoon his absent-minded reaction was, 'That's nice, dear; how long will tea be?' In his mind this was simply the latest in a long line of enthusiasms — taken up with great excitement only to be dropped a few weeks or months later. It was only when Jenny, very much a 'night owl' who had never got up before 8 a.m. in the whole of their married life, rolled out of bed in time to rouse the children *and* organize breakfast for everyone, that Paul's curiosity was aroused. At this point he began to think that this 'Jesus business' might be quite a good thing.

Sharing our faith

Good news just asks to be shared! And when you come to realize what the good news of the Christian faith is all about, it's natural to want to rush off to family and friends and tell them what they are missing. Indeed one man whom Jesus restored to life and sanity, was told to do exactly that.

> 'Go back home to your family,' Jesus said, when the man wanted to join his band of disciples, 'and tell them how much the Lord has done for you and how kind he has been to you.'
>
> *(Mark 5:19, GNB)*

Actions may speak louder than words, but there will be a time and a place for words too. When comments are made about changes in lifestyle or behaviour, we can take the opportunity to explain why, and to give Jesus the credit. It is usually a good idea to resist the temptation to preach or argue about 'the church' or 'religion'. We may have to agree to disagree about theology, but we can talk with confidence about what Jesus has done for us. If our actions and attitudes bear us out, no one can disprove that!

So far we have thought about being witnesses for Jesus to our immediate family and friends. But what about those outside our close family circle? Should we rush off to offer our services to that understaffed Sunday School, the Senior Citizens Luncheon Club, or the faithful few who distribute the church magazine? It's very easy to feel that we are only doing something that counts for God, if that something takes place outside our own home. And if the family are unresponsive or disinterested in our efforts to show them what it means to be a Christian, then it can seem much more rewarding to concentrate our efforts elsewhere.

We need to think and pray carefully, however, before we take on regular Christian activities that will keep us away from home at times when we would have previously been doing things with the family. Husbands and children are often quick to resent activities which encroach on what used to be 'their time'. And if God has given us a home and family, then that is where our first commitment has to lie. There are plenty of ways in which we can show His love within our community, which can be done quietly, but none the less effectively. The shopping done for an elderly neighbour, our readiness to go the 'extra mile' at work or simply being a listening ear to a friend or colleague in distress — all these can be done as service to the Lord, and can give opportunities to spread the good news in deed as well as word.

So much for words and actions in sharing our faith. There is another side to the equation which is even more important — prayer. It has been said that we should, 'Sometimes talk to those around us about God. But always talk to God about those around us.' This is one thing that can never be overdone. Unless we are in touch with Headquarters ourselves, we can work and talk until we are exhausted, and it will have no effect at all. But when we pray, God can work through us.

We need to pray for guidance in our actions. We need to pray too for wisdom to know when to speak and when to keep quiet. And we need to pray for the work of the Holy Spirit, to open the eyes of those we love and live amongst to their needs and His resources. What a relief it is to know that God isn't depending on you or me to make anyone a Christian. We can be a channel of His love, but we can't do the Holy Spirit's work for Him. So, essentially, sharing our faith means that we prayerfully share what we know of Jesus, in the power of the Holy Spirit, and leave the results to God. And this we can do with absolute confidence.

3

Marching To A Different Drummer

LOOKING AT LIFE FROM A MALE PERSPECTIVE

S ally and Julie were meeting over coffee. When Julie asked her whether she found it easy to share her faith with her husband, Sally replied, 'I sometimes think that Kevin is being awkward just for the sake of it. However carefully I try to explain what I believe, he either can't or won't understand. Talk about a closed mind! He won't even give it serious thought. In his view, a real man never has to admit to needing anything from anybody, so he couldn't possibly agree that he needs God, or anything that faith in God has to offer.'

'Do you think that's because most men hate to be beaten, or having to admit to being in the wrong?' queried Julie. 'Mike was taking part in a training session at work, when the all-female Accounts team beat the Rep's team (who just happened to be men), at some problem-solving task. Mike had misread the instructions at first glance, which put his team behind from the start. You'd have thought that the end of the world had come! He went on and on all evening about how badly the exercise was worded, and how faint the photo-copying was. Why can't men be more like us?'

'Why can't a man be more like...?'

Why indeed? Of course there are always exceptions that confound our carefully worked out theories, but it does seem that men and women have a different inward bias which affects the way that the sexes deal with the whole of life — spiritual matters included. And in matters of faith, it appears as if this difference can be a handicap rather than an advantage. So it's helpful to understand what it is about the masculine mindset, which can tend to work against a man becoming a Christian as an adult, particularly if his wife has beaten him to it!

From the earliest times when cavemen strode off to do battle with the local beasts and bad-hats, while his partner (we assume) kept the cave-fires burning, men have had an outward bias to their lives. Women tend to find it easier to focus on the inner life of the emotions and the spirit. They're generally more open to intuition and hunches. Perhaps this is why they seem to be more ready to hear from God and take matters of faith seriously. And when it's their husband who comes to faith first, this could be the reason that they appear to be more ready to follow suit, than when the situation is reversed.

Even as children these differences are apparent. Boys are often ahead of their sisters in physical co-ordination, and find it easier to grasp abstract ideas in Maths and Science. But they tend to outnumber the girls by three to one in remedial reading and English classes. Little girls usually talk earlier, learn to read more easily, and are more comfortable with spoken information. If this ability to deal with words is carried on into adult life — and it often is — women are automatically at a great advantage when it comes to much of our church life, which is very 'word' oriented.

Although Sally sometimes feels that she has a particularly stubborn husband, Kevin is not alone in seeing an admission of need as a sign of weakness. On the whole, men are very anxious to be seen as 'coping and competent'. And of course in the past, parents have reinforced these ideas to their sons with remarks like 'big boys don't cry'. But however desirable it may seem to be a winner in today's world — and after all, no one wants to be a loser — it does make it difficult for a man to admit that he needs God. To recognize inwardly that you've got it wrong and fallen short of God's standards is bad enough. To have to admit that you can't do anything to help yourself, or to put the situation right is even worse. And finally accepting that you really do need God's help and forgiveness can seem to be totally at odds with what you've always believed about yourself. So it's hardly surprising that it appears to be a bitter pill for Kevin and many like him to swallow.

Why won't he give church a try?

'I used to think that the day that we walked into church together would be a dream come true,' said Chrissie. 'But when it came to it, I'm not sure who was most uncomfortable — Colin or me. I'd persuaded him to come and see the children play their recorders in the Family Service, and the place was seething with women and children — the dads were definitely in the minority. Of course the service was geared towards the children, and I think the whole experience simply confirmed Colin's feeling that the church was irrelevant as far as he was concerned.'

Chrissie isn't alone in longing for her husband to join her at church. After all, if we have a loved one that we want to hear about God, the place where God's people meet and His word is taught, would seem to be the obvious place to go. But this isn't always the case.

Hostile territory?

Less than 10% of the population of Great Britain attend church regularly. For the other 90% (assuming that they don't actively practice another faith) it's a place where you may go for a christening, a wedding, or a funeral. And as the evangelist J. John says, 'On two out of the three occasions you're carried in, and don't have any say in the matter!' Church is seen by many people as a place where they feel alien and uncomfortable at best, and adrift in downright hostile territory at worst.

Of course it's hard for us to really understand this if we've been regular church-goers for a long time. We're familiar with the order of service, and at home with the way that things are done in our particular denomination. But imagine how insecure you might feel if you were a High Anglican who found herself expected to take part in a Caribbean Pentecostal church service for the first time, or a Baptist who had been invited to attend a Catholic Mass.

We're all afraid of making fools of ourselves, but men seem to be particularly reluctant to ask how things are done. If this sounds sexist, ask yourself which one of you is most likely to ask for directions when lost — you or your husband?

When the evangelist Derek Cook pointed out to a fellow minister the 'cringe' factor involved in going into the average church service for most male non-attenders, his friend was scornful. 'Men aren't so easily put off as that,' he insisted. Derek didn't argue. He simply took his colleague by the arm, and steered him out into the High Street. Pressing a £20 note into his hand, Derek told him to take it into the nearby betting shop

and wager it on any horse that took his fancy. The minister declined his kind offer! Why? Well, apart from any moral objection that he might have had to betting, there were two major reasons why he wouldn't go into a betting shop. First — someone that he knew might see him and wonder what he was up to. Second — he wouldn't know what to do when he got inside and he wouldn't want to ask for help.

'Seeker-Sensitive' services

It would be foolish to suggest that all not-yet-believing partners are put off by church services. Some accompany their husband or wife to church occasionally or regularly and are happy to do so. This is often because they have had some contact with Christian things earlier in their lives, or because they are actively seeking for God.

Occasionally those who are actually hostile find themselves confronted by God in spite of themselves. Paul speaks about this in the New Testament when he describes a situation when a non-believer just happens to come into the Christian meetings at Corinth. He is so convicted by what he sees happening and hears preached that he 'falls down and worships God, exclaiming "God is really among you."' This has been known to happen in more modern times, but unfortunately not yet with any degree of regularity in the Britain of the 1990s. We hope and pray on!

In the meantime, some churches are developing what are referred to as 'seeker-sensitive services', which are well worth looking out for, or encouraging your church to consider. On these occasions people aren't asked to sing hymns or songs expressing worship to a God that they may not yet believe in. This releases the visitors from the sense of hypocrisy which often puts up barriers in their mind. There's often drama or mime. The prayers are brief and in the talk the speaker aims to bring God's perspective to an issue of current concern or interest. It's easy to see why those who would consider themselves to be outside the church family feel more at home in this situation.

Understand where they are coming from

Although the church has a solemn responsibility to reach the world outside its door with the good news of Jesus, it's often more effective at the second stage of an individual's journey into faith, rather than the first. Of course there are conversions that happen 'out of the blue' when God meets with someone as He did with Paul on the Damascus road. But surveys show us that as many as 80% of people who come to faith do so through observing the life of a Christian friend or relative, and hearing what they have to say. What's more, they make up their minds slowly.

The Christian communicator, Max Sinclair, suggests that 'a man's instinctive reaction to the gospel is to examine it, discuss it, walk all around it and take a good look at it before he can decide what he is going to do about it.' Men need space to think things through. They also need opportunities to deal with their questions and fears without being, as one man put it, 'manipulated or emotionally mugged.' In the light of all this, you won't be surprised to hear that the average length of time it takes a seeker to move from unbelief to commitment is around four years, and of course for many it is longer.

One of the reasons for this is that many people start from a position of considerable ignorance. Fifty years ago most adults had some knowledge of the Bible and what it taught. They'd been to Sunday School as children, and Christianity was the only faith that they were likely to hear about in school. These days it's different. When a survey about the meaning of Easter was taken on the streets a couple of years ago, the ignorance among the general population was staggering. Well over half had no idea of the actual Easter story, let alone the spiritual significance of the death and resurrection of Jesus.

James Engel, in his research into attitudes to faith, worked out a scale for measuring the steps in understanding that people need to take, before they are ready to make an informed decision about the Christian faith. He begins at the point where folk have a vague sense that the supernatural exists (although most of us know some who would seem to be further away still,

ENGEL'S SCALE OF SPIRITUAL AWARENESS (adapted)			
God's Role	**Our Role**		**Understanding Level of non-believer**
General Revelation in Creation etc		-10	Awareness of supernatural
		-9	No effective knowledge of Christianity
Conviction	Presence	-8	Initial awareness
		-7	Interest
	Proclamation	-6	Aware of gospel basics
		-5	Grasp of implications
		-4	Positive attitude
	Persuasion	-3	Recognize personal problem
		-2	Challenge & decision to act.
New birth		-1	Repentance and faith
JUSTIFICATION			NEW CREATION
Growth in holiness		+1	Evaluate decision
		+2	Initial Growth
		*	Personal fruitfulness
		*	Growth in understanding
		*	Recognize spiritual gifts
		*	Growth affects actions
		*	Learns stewardship
		*	Growth in Prayer
		*	Use of spiritual gifts
		*	Witness — reproduction

and deny the existence of anything that they can't prove). Whichever of the two points you start from, he suggests that until people move on at least four stages and are interested in finding out more, it's no good preaching to them. It's during these early stages that friendship, or 'presence evangelism' is all important. Simply meeting someone to whom God is alive and relevant can make a huge impact on an unbeliever, especially if he or she is someone who lives a similar life in other ways.

Look at the 'friendship factor'

'If preaching isn't likely to help Mike that much at the moment,' said Julie, 'how on earth is he supposed to hear about God? He won't listen to me, and he hasn't got any Christian friends. The men in our church all seem to be too busy to play squash or watch football, which is what Mike does when he's not working. I don't think men have friends like women do anyway — not *real* friends. They are so self-contained and content with their little world, they give the impression that they don't need anything else.'

If this is how your husband seems, don't give up. Although many men do appear to have life all summed up, and outwardly project an image of self-reliance and indifference to spiritual things, the Bible tells us that inside they too have an emptiness which can only be filled by God. They may not recognize it themselves. They may only be aware of a vague sense of something being missing, or secretly ask themselves, 'Is this really all there is to life?' These feelings are often hastily buried under long years of the coping habit. But they do watch, and in their more thoughtful moments they do wonder why some people handle life differently.

This is where friends can come in. It's true that men

are less inclined than women to make close friends — their relationships are much more practically based. They have colleagues at work, team mates if they play sport, or neighbours with whom they're on 'nodding' terms, but they're not likely to discuss deep issues of life with any of those. And for all sorts of reasons, Christian men are generally not much better than their not-yet-believing counterparts at befriending each other.

The church is gradually becoming aware of the need for men to take the initiative in 'friendship evangelism' among their own sex, rather than leaving it to the Christian wives to cajole or badger uncommitted husbands along to church. But until this becomes the norm rather than the exception, what can we do?

- Pray that God will awaken a longing for spiritual reality within his life — you're probably doing that already!
- Pray for your partner's closest male friend or the man he most admires to come to faith — this will have a far greater impact than anything you say.
- Pray that God will stir the Christian men that your husband does know so that they become aware of his need and their responsibility to come alongside him.
- Be positive — God has a habit of working at a time and in the circumstances that we are least likely to expect.

When John attended a neighbourhood party with some reluctance, he didn't expect it to be the first step in his journey towards God. He was whiling away the time chatting idly to someone with whom he commuted to London each day, when the subject of ethics in business came up. John expressed the view that everyone 'bent the rules to some degree — it was the way things got done.' His friend disagreed, and called another man over to back his theory. John knew Peter only as the local golf professional. So he was amazed to hear him say that recently God had been showing him that it was possible to be absolutely straight in his dealings and survive financially. The spirited discussion that ensued drew the wrath of their hostess down on their heads. But before they moved on to chat to others, John had agreed to meet at Peter's home for supper the following week to pursue the matter further.

The church is gradually becoming aware of the need for men to take the initiative in 'friendship evangelism' among their own sex, rather than leaving it to the Christian wives to cajole or badger uncommitted husbands along to church.

When the time came, John wished that he had been less willing to commit himself. However, to his surprise the evening was a great success. He had an enjoyable meal with five other men — three of whom he knew fairly well and two who were comparative strangers. Three of them were quite open about their faith, and their belief that God could and did make a difference to everyday life. The other two, like John, were sceptical. After an hour of lively argument over coffee, Peter called a halt. 'We said that we'd give it an hour,' he said, 'and time is up.' John was indignant. 'We can't stop there,' he protested, 'we're just getting to grips with the thing. Can't we do this again sometime?'

And this is how John took his first steps towards

faith. For the next couple of years, the group met fairly regularly to discuss matters that were important to them all, and to explore whether a belief in God had any bearing on the subject. After a while it seemed to be a good idea to see whether the Bible had anything to say, and so the evenings gradually changed from being discussions about life, to studying the Bible. One by one, the original group of three 'don't knows' came to a real and personal faith in Christ and began to invite their friends to come and make the same discovery.

4

The Unseen Rival

THE THREAT OF CHANGE

'Get real!' Tracy just couldn't believe that men might meet to discuss the relevance of God in their business lives. The very idea seemed laughable. 'The only things that Martin would be likely to discuss with his mates are how Manchester United are doing this season, or whether he can improve the performance of our old car,' she said. 'And I can't see anyone bringing God into that! The plain fact is that he was quite happy with life as it was a year ago — or so he says. He doesn't like me being a Christian. He thinks my friends are a bunch of weirdos. He claims that the church is just after our money, and seems to hope that if he refuses to talk about it we'll gradually drift back to the way we were. He just doesn't want anything to change.'

Martin is not the only person in the world to be disturbed by change. Most of us find it quite difficult to deal with, even if it's a change that we set into motion in the first place. And if, as in Martin's experience, the change is not one that he has chosen or has any control over, and one that he views with grave suspicion, it can seem like very bad news indeed.

Psychologists tell us that as individuals we are likely to experience significant change in our lives about every seven years, as we move from one stage of life to another. But we don't move into a new situation one day, and then wake up the next morning, perfectly at home in our changed circumstances. Change is a process. People who go pot-holing don't just stroll from one cave to another underground. Caves are usually linked by passages which require a great deal of effort to negotiate. They're usually dark and cold; often narrow, rocky and uneven and sometimes wet. The pot-holers struggle through with varying degrees of effort and difficulty. Sometimes, the new cave that they discover doesn't seem anything like as spacious and interesting as the one they've left behind.

One step at a time

As we move through these transition or 'change points' in our lives, we're likely to experience a pattern of emotions which are sufficiently common for Dr Elizabeth Kubler Ross to describe them as a curve. We may not all experience them in exactly the same order, to the same degree, or for the same length of time. But in any major change we are likely to go through seven distinct stages:

Kubler Ross Change Curve

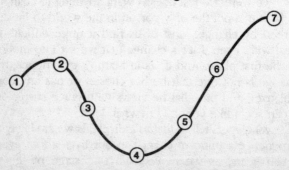

Stage One — *Shock:*
- 'I didn't know she was interested in God.'
- 'This Christianity business is taking up so much time!'
- 'He actually likes those weirdo's at the church.'

Stage Two — *Denial:*
- 'Life hasn't changed irreversibly. We can turn the clock back.'
- 'This is just another one of her enthusiasms — it will pass like all the rest have done.'
- 'It's not going to change me! I don't have to adjust *my* lifestyle or thinking!'

Stage Three — *Frustration:*
- 'It's all her fault. Why has she dragged us into this?'
- 'How am I going to cope? I just can't handle these kind of problems!'

Stage Four — *Depression:*
- 'The good times are over! All the fun has gone out of our life.'
- 'There's nothing left in our relationship — we're finished!'

When we reach stage four, we really are at the bottom of the curve, and eventually we realize that the only way to go is up. So we begin to look for ways out of the pit (although we may slip back several times) and at that point move on to:

Stage Five — *Looking for solutions:*
- We may talk to our friends, read books or magazines, or perhaps look for professional help. A new Christian might do all of those things.

Stage Six — *Make decisions:*
- When we see or hear about a way of handling our new situation, we try it out. It may not work for us, in which case we're likely to go back to Stage Five, or even Stage Four. On the other hand it may be just the solution that we are looking for. If so, we move on to:

Stage Seven — *Integrate the change into your life:*
- Safely through to acceptance! At this point the new becomes normality, and we begin to feel comfortable with life once again. It can take quite a while before this happens, and many of us slither backwards and forwards between Stages Four and Six, before we finally get a firm foothold on Stage Seven.

Lord, change me

When Tracy became a Christian she was desperate to change. She found the demands of motherhood boring and stressful, and although she loved her children she was secretly terrified that she would end up battering them. 'One week in four, Martin had to do deliveries right up to the north of Scotland,' she said, 'and he'd be away with the lorry for four or five days. By the end of the week I was having a drink to calm my nerves earlier and earlier in the day, though of course he never knew about it. When he was around, the boys didn't play up half as much, and I could manage, so it was as if I was living two lives.'

Sensing there was a problem, the health visitor suggested that Tracy took her two under-fives to the Toddler Group at the church down the road. The friends that she made there seemed to have a peace and an ability to cope with life's pressures that she envied, and Tracy began to ask questions. It wasn't very long before she too discovered that Jesus could offer the strength, comfort and company that she needed.

Tracy was surprised to discover that her husband wasn't overjoyed with the changes in her. 'I didn't expect it to affect Martin really,' she said. 'But the first thing he disliked was that I'd made friends with people he didn't know. Before that, our friends had either been people we'd been to school with, or his mates down at the Sports and Social Club. He kept saying "You don't really like those people do you?"

'Then he got mad because I wanted to take the children to the Family Service while he played football. He seemed to think I ought to prefer getting frozen in the park, and keeping the kids off the pitch, to sitting in a nice warm church. And yet he never minded if I

stayed at home and got the dinner ready instead of watching him.

'Eventually he got really depressed. He told Phil, his best mate, that he'd rather I was having an affair, because then at least he could go round and punch the other bloke on the nose. But he couldn't do much about me saying I loved someone that he couldn't see and probably didn't exist!'

Of course Martin wasn't the only one to be faced with change. Tracy wanted to change, and change she did over time. But she was shocked to discover that she wasn't cured of her short temper, or her tendency to turn to alcohol as a mood lifter, overnight. She had thought that family life would simply be an improved version of the old way of doing things. She hadn't bargained for the tensions that her wanting to be part of the church family as well would cause. Martin's reaction was completely unexpected. She felt frustrated with his apparent inability to see any value in her new approach to life, and depressed that they seemed to argue more rather than less since she had become a Christian.

'I thought that he'd be glad that I'd got some new interests and something different to talk about when he came home,' she said. 'But he acted as if I was about to run off and leave him, or give all our money to charity — which is a joke, because we've never got any spare cash anyway.'

Walk in the other man's moccasins

There's an old Indian saying to the effect that we can never expect to understand another person's point of view until we have 'walked a mile in his moccasins'. This is an excellent suggestion. But when you're trying to imagine how someone might feel when their partner has discovered a faith that they do not share, it's difficult to know what shape those 'moccasins' might be. Actions and reactions vary so much. However, the women (and the few men) who've shared their experiences with me, have all had to deal with at least one or more of the following reactions from their partner or wider family:

Jealousy

Martin saw Jesus as a rival who had 'seduced' Tracy's affections. This isn't uncommon. Christians speak of 'loving God' and they know that it is an emotion that doesn't threaten their love for their family and friends. But their partner doesn't always understand that, and perhaps we need to be more sensitive about the way we put these loyalties into words.

Mike expressed the same feeling of being excluded,

but in a slightly different way. 'I see it as if Julie had decided to adopt a baby without saying anything to me about it first,' he said. 'She brings this stranger into our home, and says "Look, isn't he wonderful? He's going to change our life, and from now on he'll be the most important person in it. His needs and opinions will come first with me, and everything I do will be geared to pleasing him. I know that you don't know anything about him as yet, but you will. And when you do, you'll think he is as perfect as I do, even though at the moment you have no desire for a child at all." And I look at this intruder who is going to take my wife's time and energy and affection, and I want to shout, "Go away — you're not wanted in my house."'

Sometimes it's the human part of the Christian family that can cause resentment and jealousy. When Chrissie became a Christian she got on very well with her minister, and he often popped in to see her. Unfortunately he chose the late afternoon to do so, and on several occasions Colin came home to find the man whom he blamed for his wife's interest in spiritual things sitting in *his* armchair, talking to *his* wife, when, in his view, she should have been getting *his* evening meal ready.

'To make matters worse, Stan wasn't a very sensitive bloke,' said Chrissie, 'and saw Colin's arrival as a great opportunity to have a chat with him. That was the last thing that Colin wanted, especially at that time of day. It got to be like one of those comedies on TV where I was shooing Stan out of the front door as Colin came in at the back. In the end I had to ask him not to come round. It was very difficult, though, because Stan really couldn't see why it should be a problem.'

Another thing that caused friction between Chrissie and Colin was the number of phone calls that she received in the evening. 'It sounded as if she was talking to a load of foreigners,' he said wryly. 'I couldn't understand half the words she was using, and I really resented her sitting in the hall listening to what I thought of as being "that load of loonies," instead of watching television with me, or chatting about my day.'

Suspicion and separation

'Before Sue became a Christian, I simply regarded the church as deadly — deadly boring!' said Steve. 'My childhood experiences as a choirboy had left me with the impression of faith as a "once a week" exercise for people with nothing better to do. But the set-up that Sue got involved with was quite different. That seemed deadly to me too, but this time deadly dangerous! I thought that she'd got herself tied up with a cult.

'First of all, they took it so seriously — there seemed to be meetings every night of the week. The services were lively, I have to admit, but they weren't read out of a book, like the ones that I'd grown up with, so you never knew where you were. And they didn't even have a church building but met in a school, or people's houses. This wasn't religion as I understood it; it was a whole new way of life. She seemed to be one of the inner circle, while I was on the outside feeling more and more cut off from her.'

Fear and anger

Negative emotions are closely interlinked, and when we are afraid we often become angry as well. One of the results of Chrissie's coming to faith, was that she handled things differently in her day-to-day life. Previously a very nervous young woman who consulted her husband about everything, and who panicked when a situation arose which she couldn't handle easily, she became more relaxed and confident.

'When the washing machine went wrong and flooded the whole of the ground floor, I was upset of course,' she said, 'but instead of flying to the phone and ringing Colin for advice, I just cleared up the mess, and arranged for the engineer to call. I thought that he would be really pleased, but he was angry and accused me of not caring about our possessions that had been spoilt. And the fact that I'd arranged for the machine to be mended without consulting him first didn't go down too well either.'

Colin admitted that he'd been unreasonable, but realized with hindsight that his anger stemmed from fear. He was afraid that Chrissie didn't need him any more, and that his role in her life was being taken over by God. This made him feel rejected and very insecure.

Apathy

'If you want to believe it then that is OK for you, but please leave me out of it. I want nothing to do with your church or your God.' Variations on this theme are by far the most common reaction to the new faith of one partner from the not-yet-believing husband or wife. And although it's less painful to deal with than outright hostility, it's often the mask behind which a frightened or puzzled person is hiding, and needs to be appreciated as such.

'When Simon was a toddler,' said Louise, 'he had an infuriating way of dealing with anything he didn't want to hear. He would squat down on his haunches, pull his sweater up over his head and curl up into as small a ball as he could. Then he would put his fingers in his ears and hum! I sometimes think that that is what his father does mentally when I say anything about the church or Christianity. Pete simply blocks it out because he is afraid that if he listened he would be challenged to react in some way.'

Challenged to react! Some people love a challenge, but most of us are like Pete — we approach the unknown very cautiously! We have already seen how difficult the process of change is to handle. Consciously or unconsciously, most of us shape our values, beliefs and attitudes from the things that we learned from our parents, or those who cared for us as children. These become so much part of us, that to have those values and beliefs challenged is uncomfortable. If we allow ourselves to think differently, we might find that the foundations on which we have built our lives are undermined. Then perhaps we would need to change — and that is risky. So the safe option is to cling tightly to the old. If we don't take risks, we're not likely to fail. And if we don't fail, we won't look stupid — which, as we have already seen, is very important to most people and particularly to men.

5

I Need Somebody

THE STRUGGLE OF THE 'LONE' CHRISTIAN

'It's all very well,' said Jenny indignantly, 'to tell me that I must put myself in my husband's shoes, and see things from his point of view. I know that I'm the one who has set all these changes in motion, and so I need to understand the effect that it's having on my family. But what about me? Who's going to love and understand me? Who's going to stand by me when I feel down in the dumps? Who's going to help me to adjust to the changes in *my* life?'

Becoming a Christian or recommitting your life to God as an adult does have far reaching consequences. As we've already seen, the not-yet-believing partner will have a lot of adjusting to do, but they are not the only ones. Any new Christian will have a great deal to learn about faith and its practice. But if you're the lone Christian in your family, you might also find yourself battling with the sense of being isolated at home, *and* with being different within your church in subtle, but none the less testing, ways.

Take a look at the line drawing in the Good News Bible with which the artist Annie Vallotton illustrates the invitation of Jesus to 'Come to Me, all of you who are tired from carrying heavy loads, and I will give you rest.' (*Matthew 11:28*).

Come to me, all of you who are tired.

God's enemy, Satan, constantly taunts and attacks God's children, and often he does it through sheer weariness. So which of those figures do you identify with? Do you feel bowed down with your concern for your family, or a dismal failure in your attempt to share your faith with them? Perhaps you feel like the man on crutches — handicapped because you are a lone Christian rather than one of a couple or a family group. Maybe you long to be a child again, safe in someone's arms, but at the moment you seem to be an onlooker, wistfully watching from the sidelines.

All the great men and women of faith seem to have fallen flat on their faces at some time in their lives.

A group of women who looked at that picture with me, found that it provoked those reactions and others beside. We all respond differently, but knowing that, as Louise put it, 'Jesus comes in when the whole world goes out' takes away the sting of loneliness. And sometimes just hearing how others have been assailed by the same feelings and fears and have survived helps us to cope.

'I make such a mess of things'

Louise's face was pale and she looked as if she had been crying. We were meeting in her home to plan the church drama group's part in the Christmas services. 'I don't think I should be involved in this!' she said, heaving a huge sigh. 'No one in our family is talking to one another tonight, and it's mostly my fault. Pete's parting shot as he went out was, "Call yourself a Christian after that performance?" and I just wanted to curl up and die. What can I possibly say to anyone about Jesus when I make such a mess of things? It's sheer hypocrisy!'

Jenny nodded sympathetically. 'I shouldn't think that anyone would come to the Carol Service from work after seeing me in action today,' she confessed. 'First of all, I forgot to set the alarm so I arrived late. That meant that my boss went off to a board meeting without the set of papers which arrived for him, via me, in the internal post. He was not a happy man — and let me know it.

'I was being a martyr — working through my lunch hour to catch up — and missed Moira's leaving "do" so I felt really fed up. I was just grabbing a sandwich and a cup of coffee at my desk when the others came back, and Teresa caught my mug with her bag, tipping coffee all over the report that I'd just finished. She is *so* clumsy. It didn't really matter that much: I only had to clear up the mess and print out another copy. But I really flipped and told her what I thought about her — she's been getting on my nerves for weeks. She ended up in the Ladies in floods of tears, and you could have cut the atmosphere in the office with a knife for the rest of the afternoon. It really spoiled Moira's last day, and I feel so guilty.'

'I lost my temper with Grandad...'

'I nagged the children about their bedrooms again, even though we'd agreed...'

'I vowed I wouldn't gossip, and yet before I knew it we had shredded her reputation over lunch...'

'He was late again and I thumped his dinner down on the table so hard that the plate cracked...'

We all had confessions to make that evening! It had obviously been one of those weeks. And the worst part about it was that, as always, we had broken our best resolutions in front of the very people who mattered most to us — our families; our friends; our workmates. All those people who were likely to link the reality of our faith with the quality of our behaviour.

Of course, stories of failure amongst those who try to walk in God's ways are nothing new — the Bible is full of them. All the great men and women of faith seem to have fallen flat on their faces at some time in their lives. They grumbled about what God asked them to do and where he led them. Moses doubted God; King David committed adultery; and in Peter's case, he even denied any connection with Jesus, the one whom he'd promised to follow to the gates of death itself.

No failure is final with God

What a relief it is to know that there's always a way back. Jesus warned Peter that he was likely to deny him. 'I have pleaded in prayer for you,' He said, 'that your faith should not completely fail. So when you have repented and turned to me again, strengthen and build up the faith of your brothers.' But Peter, full of self-confidence would have none of it. 'I am ready to die for you!' he declared. A few hours later, in answering a servant girl, he was cursing and insisting that he had nothing to do with Jesus at all.

Have you ever tried to imagine how Peter must have

felt when, on his way out to flogging and death, Jesus turned and quietly looked at him? There was no furious reminder of his rash words, hurled over the heads of the gawping onlookers. No cutting 'I told you so.' But in that instant Peter realized what he had done, and 'he went outside and wept bitterly'.

It could have all ended there, but we know that it didn't. When Jesus rose from the dead, He sent an individual message to Peter, to make sure that he felt himself included in the group of disciples summoned to meet Jesus. And once Peter had reaffirmed his love and commitment, Jesus gave him an important job to do, with no warnings about 'not blowing it this time'.

Thankfully Peter is not a special case. The Bible tells us that Jesus is praying for us too. And when we do make a mess of things, the moment we turn back to God He is standing with open arms, ready to gather us close to His heart once again. There's no probationary period, to see whether we have 'learned our lesson this time'; forgiveness is immediate and absolute. And what is more, we are not disqualified from serving God — in fact, we are commanded to do so, hopefully with more understanding and sympathy for people's failings.

'I'm sorry, I was in the wrong — please forgive me.' These are ten of the most difficult words in the world. They certainly seem to stick in our throats, especially when, having said them to God, we then have to go and say them to the person that we have offended. Many people seem to work on the principle of 'never apologize, never explain'. So if Christians admit to being in the wrong and ask for their forgiveness they are often both surprised and challenged.

That is a comfort to me. Of course, we want to demonstrate the reality of our faith in the way we live our day to day lives. But when we fail, our readiness to apologize and put things right as far as we're able, can be a powerful witness to the power and grace of God in action. It doesn't mean that it will be easy to do, but the Holy Spirit can, and will, enable us to do what would be impossible in our own strength, if we ask Him.

'I'm all on my own'

'After a week when life at home has been difficult,' said Clare, 'I might manage to get up on Sunday without upsetting Robin by setting the alarm too early, clear up the breakfast things, prepare the lunch…and I leave the house telling myself that I'm coping well. Then, after all that effort, I get to the church door and have to force myself to go in alone. Sometimes the sight of all those families sitting together is almost more than I can bear.'

Of course Clare isn't the only lone woman in her church, even though she sometimes feels it. A conservative estimate suggests that there are at least 500,000 women in Britain whose husbands don't share their faith. Add to this the men whose wives are uncommitted, and the Christians of either sex, whose partner is at this moment 'following from afar' or even denying the faith he or she once professed, and you can see that Christians who are spiritually 'single' form a sizeable minority in any church.

If you go to a large church like Clare does, however, it can be very difficult to locate others who are in the same situation. After she'd asked the organist's wife whether her husband ever came to church (and was told that he might as well have his bed there!) she decided to ask her vicar if he knew of any other women who came to church on their own.

'He suggested that Josie, Carmen, Doris and I met him for coffee at the vicarage one evening,' said Clare, 'and it was wonderful. Just talking to someone who knew how I felt was such a relief. We decided to meet once a month and called our group Caseo — which stands for 'Come And Support Each Other'. We didn't have our meetings announced, but gradually the word got round, and now there are sixteen women who meet, although not everyone can make it every time. It doesn't stop me from getting a lump in my throat when I see a couple walk in to church, but it's wonderful to have other people to share my joys and sorrows with, and to know that they are praying for my husband too.'

'I'm a second-class citizen in the eyes of the church'

'I often think,' said Donna, 'that there are three types of Christians in our church. There are those who can be involved up to the hilt — attending every service, volunteering for every need, giving to every good cause — and do it all with gusto. There are those who could be doing all those things, but choose not to — for reasons of their own. And then there are those like me who would love to be totally involved but can't be. I get really hurt when I'm lumped in with the "coulds but don'ts" by the "cans and do's". I overheard the leader of the Stewarding Team say to one of her cronies, "It's no good asking Donna Reynolds to go on the rota, because she's not committed to the church. She isn't here every Sunday, I'm afraid."

'I was so angry. I wanted to shout at her "Have you any idea how hard it is to get here as often as I do? I'd give my right arm to have my husband up at the front of the church leading worship, like yours is — instead of digging his allotment or wanting me at home to help him with the decorating."

'I would love to be a steward,' she went on sadly,

'because I know what a difference a warm welcome at the door makes if you arrive on your own. But I was never asked, and I couldn't volunteer, could I, knowing what they thought of me?'

Donna is a gentle and sensitive person, and that experience makes her feel more unkindly judged than she really is by the majority of people in her church (although this doesn't excuse the lack of sensitivity shown by the one or two). She didn't stop going to church, but the knock to her confidence was so great, that it was a long time before she felt able to respond to any requests for help in the church.

This sensitivity to thoughtless remarks comes out strongly in a book by an American author, Linda Davis. She, too, was hurt by an insensitive remark — this time about women who were at church too much, instead of at home, with their unsaved husbands 'where they belonged'. She shed bitter tears in private and wondered if she should be staying away if her presence offended people, but she chose not to respond in that way:

> I was presented with a turning point in my
> Christian life. I could choose to give up fighting
> the constant…pressures of being an unequally
> yoked wife and drop out of the established
> church…Or I could receive God's tender healing,
> remembering that Jesus felt every one of my
> wounds as He hung on the cross. Then I could
> pick myself up, dust myself off, charge back into
> the church with all my might and say 'Jesus is my
> Lord too!' I'm glad that I chose to do the latter…
> Why? Because many years later that is where my
> husband experienced new birth in Jesus Christ
> himself, forever changing his [and our] life.
>
> (From *How to be the Happy Wife of an Unsaved Husband*)

It is fatally easy to be so thoughtless or lacking in understanding that we really damage one another in the process. We need to be very aware of Satan's efforts to disrupt and destroy in this way. And we also need to hang on to the fact that although human beings may at times mistakenly value people for what they do, rather than for who they are, God has no such favourites. He loves us just because we are us, and knows our circumstances perfectly.

So when we're tempted to label ourselves (or worse still, label others) as 'also-rans' in the Christian race, because of what we can or can't do within the church, let's remember the prophet Samuel in the Old Testament. He was sent by God to anoint one of Jesse's sons as the king to follow Saul, but God did not tell him ahead of time which young man had been chosen. While Samuel was trying to work it out, even he, godly

He loves us just because we are us.

man that he was, was influenced by their looks. But God said,

> 'I don't make decisions the way you do. Men judge by outward appearances, but I look at a man's thoughts and intentions.'
>
> *I Samuel 16:*7, Living Bible

'It's my fault that he doesn't believe'

'Love him into the Kingdom, my dear,' boomed Mrs Markham, whose husband Walter had been a lay preacher for forty years. 'If we love enough, those walls of resistance just come tumbling down.'

'Can't she see,' said Debbie with understandable bitterness, 'that it's just *because* I love Bill so much that I long for him to become a Christian? But I can't love his mind into accepting what he refuses even to contemplate!'

This is one of the most difficult areas that any Christian has to handle. To want to share our faith with those nearest and dearest to us is the most natural thing in the world. But a parent cannot force a child to believe, however carefully he or she has been taught, however good a parental example has been set, and however much he or she has been loved. And the same is equally so with an adult. We are *not* responsible for the faith, or lack of it, of any other individual. To take on that responsibility is to burden ourselves with something that we have not been asked to carry.

Of course, we do have a responsibility to live in such a way that we are good advertisements for the faith that we profess — and sometimes we'll fail. We'll ask God to love the person we love through us — and sometimes we'll be imperfect channels, because we are still imperfect people. But God knows that, and He will use us in spite of ourselves, if we'll allow Him to.

As well as our living and our loving, the Bible tells us to make the effort to think through what we believe. This is so that, as the apostle Peter instructs the early church, we'll 'be ready at all times to answer anyone who asks you to explain the hope that you have in you.' *(1 Peter 3:15)* But notice that we're told to *answer* when we are *asked*, and then to 'do it with gentleness and respect.' And that is really where our responsibility ends. We can pray, act lovingly and answer questions when the opportunity arises. But beyond that everyone has to take responsibility for the choices they make, and ultimately that choice can only lie between each individual and God.

6

Made In Heaven?

GOD'S PLAN FOR MARRIAGE

'The trouble with marriage today,' said Chrissie, 'is that people expect so much from it. My mum and dad's generation were much more realistic. When they got married they knew pretty much what was likely to happen. Dad would go out to work and earn the money; Mum would run the home and bring up the family. If there was enough to eat, the kids stayed healthy and kept out of trouble, and you had a night out once a year on your wedding anniversary, you had a good marriage.'

It's true that there are fewer certainties in the 1990s, for all sorts of reasons. Life *has* changed. Men and women's expectations of marriage, and what they should expect from one another, are different even from twenty years ago. For one thing, with so many marriages ending in divorce, a whole generation has grown up questioning whether there is any point in getting married in the first place. And even if they plan to marry eventually, they may have had few role models of happy long-term relationships on which to base their thinking.

Because of this, marriages have often been (and still are) built on very shaky foundations. We may well have spent a year or more planning the dress, the flowers and the refreshments for the wedding day. But as we tread softly down the aisle, or step hopefully into the Registrar's office, many of us have only the vaguest of visions of what we expect from the institution of marriage. And once married, we have even less idea of how we might bring it about.

Dream lovers?

None of us get married intending to be unhappy, and most of us expect to have all our needs completely met in this relationship. It's unrealistic, but we all do it! 'Once I've tied the knot with Mr Right', we tell ourselves, 'I'll be okay.' Perhaps we have a mental picture of the husband or wife that is our 'ideal'. The way that this picture takes shape depends on many factors.

A girl is more influenced than she may realize by what her father was like. If they had a good relationship, she is liable to model her ideal man on him. If he was distant or unloving, then she will be drawn to a man with very different characteristics. Film and television heroes and those from romantic novels will also combine to shape her 'dream lover', whom she is sure will wonderfully meet her particular needs, and complement her character. And the same situation applies with a man and his mother.

While we may realize at the outside that our real-life partner has a few of the 'ideal' characteristics missing from his make-up, we think, blithely, that within the framework of marriage we can make the one or two alterations necessary. What we often do not realize is that our partner may have the same plans for us!

Of course, over the years both individuals within the relationship change to a greater or lesser degree. We are steadily being moulded by circumstances, and the pressures exerted by our partner. This is true for all marriages, whether we are actively seeking God's will for our lives, whether we have no faith, or whether our relationship becomes a 'mixed marriage' in the sense that one comes to faith or renews a Christian commitment which the other doesn't share. But it is within this third scenario that the pressures are likely to be the greatest, because there is a 'third party' in the relationship, who wasn't there when the couple started out together.

Does God make a difference?

'If I had your husband,' she said, fixing me with a steely stare, 'I would think that I was in heaven on earth.' I bristled slightly at the implied possibility of 'husband-napping' and then realized what she meant. It wasn't *my* husband in particular that she was longing for — wonderful man though he is — but a husband who shared her faith. In Donna's mind at that moment was the equation: "Myself plus Christian husband equals perfect marriage and a life lived happily ever after.'

I guess that Donna isn't alone in believing that, but I'm afraid that she is assuming too much. Of course many marriages in which both partners are Christian *are* very happy. It certainly builds in a strong foundation when you both have the same view of what is important in life. If you agree on what you want to put first, it reduces the likelihood of strains occurring because the two halves of a couple are pulling in different directions.

The Bible even says that a marriage in which both partners are allowing the love of God to rule in their lives, is a living picture of the relationship that exists between Jesus and the church. Jesus is pictured as the bridegroom who was prepared to die in order to woo and win the one he loves. All the men and women who have believed in Him across the world and throughout the ages are seen as his bride. What a challenge and a goal to aim for! Our relationships have the potential within them to reflect that degree of self-giving love!

But in spite of all the wonderful possibilities that there are in a marriage, especially between a man and a woman who love God and one another, there is nothing automatic about it. And a man who comes to share the faith that his wife already professes (or vice versa) won't inevitably become any more of an ideal partner overnight. Marriage is a relationship that may have been designed in heaven, but it very definitely has to be built on earth. Togetherness has to be worked at: day after day, month after month, year after year. Shared belief will certainly oil the wheels, but it won't act as an automatic pilot to guide us unswervingly to married bliss.

What is a 'Christian' marriage?

'If you are saying that God doesn't give you any guarantees,' said Sally, 'even if you are both active Christians, does that mean that those of us with unbelieving partners have even less of a chance of happiness? There must be a difference in a relationship where both of you take God into account, but does that mean that those of us who are 'solo' believers have a second-class marriage? What is a 'Christian' marriage anyway? Even though Kevin doesn't seem to believe much these days, he wanted to get married in church as much as I did, so I reckon he would say that we had a Christian marriage.'

Sally was raising a very important — and difficult — question. What makes a marriage a 'Christian' one? Is it the building that decides it? The fact that the ceremony took place in a church, rather than a Registrar's Office, a temple or a mosque? Or is the crucial fact that the couple, their family and friends met together 'in the sight of God', and took their vows in His name? Where does the personal belief (or lack of it) of the bride and groom themselves come in — both at the time of the wedding and on into the years that lie ahead?

The Bible doesn't appear to deal with this particular issue in detail. Surprisingly perhaps, there is no concise attempt to define the kind of marriage God approves of, apart from the fact that His people in the Old Testament were forbidden to intermarry with the heathen tribes around them. The Old Testament speaks of marriage frequently, but we are not told any details of how or where the Jewish ceremony was carried out or what life was like for the couple afterwards.

In the New Testament, many of the first Christians would have been married when they first came to faith, and not all of them had partners who converted with them. However there are some general principles that we *can* gather from the Bible. Here are some of them:

- **Marriage is God's gift to us.** He planned it to meet our need for human love and companionship and to give us a secure framework for the joyful expression of our sexuality. *(Genesis 2:18, 24)*
- **As unmarried Christians,** we are to seek a partner who shares our faith. *(2 Corinthians 6:14)*
- **In a marriage where only one of the couple comes to faith,** God is very definitely present. Because of the believing partner's trust and obedience, God regards the relationship as valid, and one that He can bless. *(1 Corinthians 7:12-14)*
- **If we find ourselves married to an unbeliever,** that is not, in itself, a reason for us to walk out

on the relationship, or to deny our partner sexual intimacy. *(1 Corinthians 7:3)*

- **If the unbelieving partner leaves,** in spite of our best efforts to be a good husband or wife, he or she is free to do so. *(1 Corinthians 7:15)*

This doesn't really help us to decide whether the relationship we are in could be called 'Christian' or not, but maybe that isn't the point. Perhaps we need to be more concerned about whether, as Christians, we're living in accordance with the intentions that God has for marriage. Discovering how we can be the best partner that we can possibly be, within our particular relationship, is probably far more important than any label that we or others might choose to pin on it.

What is God's purpose for my marriage?

Each of us is unique and special; not one of us has the same finger-prints as anyone else. And because we are all different, our marriage relationships are bound to be equally varied. But although we may have very dissimilar experiences of life, God has created us all, men and women alike, with certain things in common. We have:

- the same basic needs in our lives;
- the same distinct dimensions to our lives;
- the same responsibilities to God, to each other, and for the next generation.

And however we may work it out in practice, God has designed marriage to be a relationship within which it is possible for both partners:

- to have those needs met more completely;
- to develop our potential in each dimension more fully;
- to carry out our responsibilities more effectively.

We shall have a look at God's plan for us as parents a little later on, but let's look first at how marriage lived according to God's pattern can make it easier for our needs to be met and our potential to be developed.

Meeting our God-given needs

As we have seen earlier, we are all born with certain needs. And although we may not realize it, much of what we do, both in marriage and in our lives generally, is driven by a desire to have those needs met.

Our most basic need of all is to survive. Unless we start out in life with food, water, heat and shelter, we won't live long enough to get married. These survival needs stay with us throughout life. Once we have obtained what we need for mere existence, the next most powerful force in our lives is the need to feel secure. We also need to feel loved and that we belong. We need to feel that our being alive has significance within our own small world. And once we have these things as firm foundations under our feet, we all want to achieve things, and to be successful. The strength of that desire varies from person to person, but to some degree we all have a need to be accepted and recognized as someone who has a valuable contribution to make.

Marriage — a new life and a new loyalty

When we are children our survival and security needs are met by our parents, or those who have the responsibility for bringing us up. As we grow up, God intends that we should learn to give and receive love from those closest to us. Within this small circle of relationships, most of our views about ourselves, other people and the world in which we live are formed. Hopefully we will be encouraged and helped to succeed with the tasks we undertake and the challenges we face as we grow up. Then, as adults, we usually move on to marriage.

Within marriage we become part of a new support system. We now work at making a home with our partner, co-operating to make sure that our survival needs are met. We also have learned to express love and encouragement to one another, supporting and applauding each others' efforts to achieve.

In order to do this well, we have to recognize that childhood and the independence of the single life is behind us. We now have an entirely new life and loyalty to which we need to be committed. In the book of Genesis we read that this involves two steps — often called 'leaving and cleaving'.

When we marry, we *leave* our parents and the wider family in which we have grown up, both physically and emotionally. We need to realize that we are doing this, and do it publicly. This is why the wedding ceremony is important, and where those who simply live together miss a key step in their relationship.

At weddings that are held at my church, the minister reminds the parents that their children are about to set up a new family unit. He asks them if they understand this, and will do all that they can to work with the bride and groom in the adjustments that they will all need to make.

The second step is described in older versions of the Bible as *cleaving* to our husband or wife. That word always makes me think of a limpet on a rock. The more modern versions speak of being *united*, but whatever word we use, the feeling is of becoming so closely bound to our partner, that in a sense we are like one person. 'Bone of my bones and flesh of my flesh,' exclaimed Adam as he welcomed Eve into his life. This is now the relationship which is to be put before all others. In the words of the Anglican service, we promise that 'forsaking all others' we shall 'be faithful...as long as we both shall live.'

A new source of strength

When I was a small child, we had a large elm tree growing opposite our dining-room window. In the spring the rooks were a wonderful source of meal-time entertainment as they built their nests with a great deal of flapping and cawing! A favourite labour-saving device that the birds employed, was to wait until a neighbouring pair had flown off to forage for twigs and then steal the material from the absentees' half-built nest. Eventually one pair, with more brainpower than the rest, got wise to what was going on! One of them stood guard over their home-to-be, while the other one flew off for supplies. They knew by instinct what the author of Ecclesiastes meant when he observed

> Two are better off than one because together they can work more effectively. If one falls down, the other can help him up...If it is cold, two can sleep together and stay warm...two can resist an attack that would defeat one...   *Ecclesiastes 4:9-12*

A good marriage has the potential for being the best support system known to man — and woman! We belong; we are of first importance in someone else's life, and we have promised to be there for one another, sticking to our partner through thick and thin. As my aunt said to me on the evening before I got married, 'Remember dear, from now on it is you two against the world.'

Remember — it's the two of us against the world.

Fulfilling our God-given potential

We are all born with certain distinct dimensions to our lives. I imagine them as the different faces of a prism; they are separate and definite and yet they flow into one another. In order to be a 'whole person' we need to develop and enjoy our potential in four areas:

- our physical life;
- our mental or intellectual life;
- our emotional life — which will include our relationships;
- our spiritual life.

As we look at ourselves and other people, we can see that we don't always grow in each area equally. But one of our tasks in marriage is to do all that we can to help our partners to fulfil their potential. The final goal is that at the end of life we are both more complete as people, than we were when we stepped out together.

At the beginning of this chapter, we looked at the fact that human marriage can be a picture of Jesus' relationship with His bride, the church. The reason that He loved her and laid down His life for her (and we are all included in that if we are His followers) is explained in the letter to the Ephesians, where Paul writes:

> **Christ loved the church and gave His life for it...in order to present the church to Himself in all it's beauty — pure and faultless, without spot, wrinkle or any other imperfection.**

In one sense, that is a picture that can only apply to Jesus. He can do that for us, as individuals, because He is God. There is no way in which we can impose growth or wholeness on our husband or wife, however much we love them. And often, because we are human beings who fail, we are selfish, and more concerned with getting than giving. But, if we allow God to work through us, we can make it easier for our partner to grow into the person that God wants him or her to be. It can happen in what seems to be the most unpromising of situations.

Take Hilary and Hugh's marriage, for example. Hilary was very disappointed in her marriage. Her husband was withdrawn and seemed to lack any interest in her or their children. He rarely talked to her, except to grumble, and he was openly critical of her faith. One day as she phoned her vicar in despair for counsel and comfort, she had the strangest experience.

'It was a most extraordinary thing,' she said. 'I was pouring out my problems when this picture came into my mind. I would hardly dare to call it a vision, but it was a picture of such extraordinary clarity and colour that I lost the thread of what I was saying completely. In it, Hugh was walking up the path to meet me. But it wasn't the rather silent and miserable man that I knew. He was glowing with life and happiness; laughing and reaching out his arms to a group of people standing nearby. As I watched, God spoke to me with absolute clarity.

"'This is the man that I am wooing and long to win,' God said, "and this is what he can become. I have called you into this relationship to be a channel of My love. Through you I will help and heal him. Together you can build something beautiful for Me.'"

7

If That's Marriage – It's Not As I Know It!

REVIEWING YOUR MARRIAGE; RENEWING YOUR COMMITMENT

A group of us had met to discuss the topic of marriage and how we could begin to live out God's ideals for it. As she introduced the subject Lorna read a quotation:

> The amount of satisfaction you get from marriage is determined in large part by how well you and your partner...meet certain of each others' needs. It also depends on the degree of opportunity you have, and encouragement you get from one another, to meet some of your own needs.
>
> *No Fault Marriage*, Marcia Laswell & Norman Lobsenz.

'It would be wonderful,' said Clare dreamily, 'if marriage could really be like that. Helping and supporting one another — not just on the surface with the day to day things but deep down. Knowing one another through and through. But let's be realistic. Robin is too busy keeping the shop going so that we survive financially to worry about anything else. And I'm not sure that I even know what my own needs are — let alone his.'

The rest of us seemed to have a rather clearer idea

of what we wanted than Clare did, for Lorna had barely finished asking, 'What would you say you wanted more than anything else from your marriage?' when the answers came flying back.

'A friend — someone who really *wants* to share everything with me.'

'I wish he'd tell me that I did *some* things right, and back me up in front of others, rather than criticizing me all the time.'

'A lover — who's a good listener too!'

'A real father for the kids.'

'I'd like to think that I came first with him — just sometimes.'

'David is very caring and concerned when I'm ill, but when I'm fit, he just seems to expect me to cope with everything. Some day to day support would be wonderful.'

'Someone who will share in the responsibilities of our marriage — not leave all the decisions to me and then blame me when things turn out in a way he doesn't like.'

A number of heads nodded in agreement with that statement.

'A husband who shares my faith — so that we are wanting the same things from life.'

That comment had unanimous support too!

After the first rush of ideas, there was silence for a few minutes while we thought about the reality of marriage. Quietly we compared what we had experienced with what God intended for this relationship. There was so much potential for joy and disappointment. Finally, Julie said rather sadly,

'I'm not sure that I find all this talk about having my needs met and walking shoulder to shoulder through life very helpful. I feel like a child peering into the shop window at Christmas time, looking at all the lovely things on display and knowing that hardly any of them are likely to come my way.'

Dream on!

Life doesn't always measure up to our dreams, does it? The reality that we experience, can be very painful. When we hear that God's ideal for the first man and woman was total commitment — meeting each other's needs and complementing each other's personality — it at first seems like a wonderful goal to aim at. But when we think about it a bit more deeply, we may come up with other reactions.

A few of us may assume that a perfect marriage is something to be slipped on with the wedding rings — and feel bitter and cheated when it isn't. Others look at friends who seem to be doing better in the 'Happy Marriage Stakes' and wonder what the magic formula is, which they have so far failed to discover. And many people look at the relationship that they have, and are tempted to give up in despair. 'All this giving and togetherness might have been an option in the Garden of Eden,' we tell ourselves, 'but in the 1990s with all our pressures — impossible!'

There is some truth in all of those reactions. In a perfect world, we would all be able to love and care for one another perfectly. But in our imperfect world, our lives are spoiled by sin on every level. If God created us with these needs, then He must also intend them to be met, at least to some degree. But He works only with our co-operation and consent. And in our 'Me First' and 'Be happy at all costs' culture, laying down our lives for one another isn't something that comes naturally — if it ever did!

So how do we work at making our marriages the

best they can be? 'If Kevin was a Christian,' said Sally, 'he might not live up to what the Bible teaches all the time, any more than I do. But we would both be at church on a regular basis, hearing teaching on how we should live. We would both be open to what God wants for our marriage, and we would both have the Holy Spirit to help us. As things are, I feel sometimes as if our relationship is like a barrel that I'm pushing up a hill. If I stop making an effort, it will roll back and squash us all flat.'

Sally is quite right. We do need the Holy Spirit's help in our marriage, as in every other part of our life, if we are to function according to the 'Maker's Instructions'. And if our partner doesn't share our faith, it is obviously going to be that much more of a challenge. But even if Kevin comes to faith, as Sally prays he will, she can only be responsible for *her* actions and reactions. She can't make him God's 'Ideal Christian Husband' but she can do her utmost to grow into God's ideal for a wife. So even if we don't have a partner who is interested in God's pattern for marriage, we can still work at improving our own performance as God's woman (or man) for our particular situation, by giving time and thought to what could be called the Five R's:

- Review how we are doing at the moment;
- Revise our ideas of what we would like to happen;
- Renew our commitment to do whatever is necessary;
- Receive all the help God has to offer;
- Refine the skills that we will need.

We will look at all these areas in the rest of this book, but before we can decide where we want to go, or how we may have to change things in order to get there, we need to take a look at where we are now.

Reviewing — satisfied or struggling?

Psychologists who specialize in marital relationships say that every marriage has three stages. Which one reflects your experience at the moment?

Are you still enjoying the 'Honeymoon stage' where romantic love gives a glow to everything and husband and wife float on a cloud of togetherness (touching down occasionally for a minor difference of opinion which is rapidly resolved). This may last for as short a time as five weeks or as long as five years — and for most of us it will end somewhere in the middle of that period.

Or are you well into the 'Facing Reality' stage where faults tend to come into sharp focus? Are you reacting with what you hope are a few subtle attempts at remodelling your partner? This is generally a rather fruitless activity, and when it fails, conflict and confrontation often follow.

The third stage is where we all end up sooner or later. It might be called 'Make or Break'. We can give up at this point and resign ourselves to a life of continuing arguments, increasing estrangement or even divorce. Or we make a conscious decision to adjust to reality and do the very best we can with it.

How would you rate the 'satisfaction factor' in your marriage on a scale of 1 – 10? If you are reading this book you will almost certainly have a roof over your head and the absolute necessities of clothing, food and warmth will have been met. Otherwise you could well be tearing the book up to make a fire, or pawning it with other possessions to raise some money for a loaf of bread! Accepting that, are you and/or your partner earning enough to pay the bills and give you a sense of security? Or is there constant gnawing anxiety — and perhaps rows — about making ends meet?

And what about the 'love quotient'? The heady days of drifting along on cloud nine may have gone, but do you feel loved and accepted for the person you are now? Do you gain a sense of satisfaction and achievement from the activities that fill your daily life? How do you think your partner would answer those same questions?

Are you still enjoying the 'Honeymoon stage' where romantic love gives a glow to everything and husband and wife float on a cloud of togetherness (touching down occasionally for a minor difference of opinion which is rapidly resolved)

As we've already seen, every individual and every relationship is unique and special, and constantly changing, even though those changes may be small and hardly noticeable at the time. But the general foundation of marriage needs to be the same for all of us if we are to build a secure and lasting structure. So have you both left your childhood family, emotionally and physically? Not with any sense of abandoning those whom you still have a responsibility to love and respect, but having a new priority and focus? And are you committed to building one another up in every dimension of your lives — separately and together. Are you a good team — giving and receiving mutual support?

Revising — where are we going?

'It's all very well to talk about being a team,' said Donna, 'but that means that you need more than one player. How can you have a team-type relationship when only one of you wants to be in it? David has his own life-plans, and he expects me to fit in with those, either by joining in with him or coping with the family while he does his own thing.'

David is not unique in his attitude to marriage. Different people feel comfortable with varying degrees of closeness to other people. This is influenced by a number of things. First, our own experience of family life — we tend to either reproduce or firmly reject what we saw our parents do. Then there is our own temperament — some people seem to need a greater amount of personal space than others. And the final and major factor is whether we are men or women. Men tend to see marriage as a comfortable and important base from which to go out and live the rest of their lives. Women are looking for emotional and spiritual intimacy. We could show these degrees of closeness by a diagram, in which we see our partner as a Soulmate, Workmate and Flatmate:

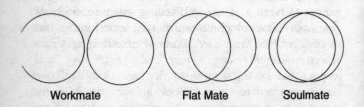

Workmate   Flat Mate   Soulmate

David would identify with the idea of having a Workmate. Although he is content to be married, he is essentially quite a solitary person. He sees being independent and self-sufficient as the marks of a 'real' man. He has never learned how to share his feelings at any depth, and finds the idea of too much 'togetherness' oppressive. So he wants to live a fairly separate life, but still have the pleasure and comfort of sharing some things with his wife. Donna, like many women, is really longing for a Soulmate — a partner with whom she can share everything, including the spiritual dimension of her life.

As David feels uncertain whether there is a God, and doesn't care much either way at the moment, it's unlikely that either of them can meet the other's ideal completely. They may both have to be prepared to compromise and do their best to meet one another somewhere in the middle. This kind of marriage is rather like having a Flatmate. It's an intimate relationship, in which you share practical things, making a very definite effort to support one another emotionally, but not demanding more than the other feels able to give.

Renewing our commitment

'Having a Flatmate sounds rather…well…flat!' said Jenny. 'A grey sort of nothingness, where neither of you really gets what you want. That seems like a bad deal all round to me. Can't God do something better for us than that?'

I suppose the answer to that question is that it depends what you are expecting Him to do! In the Anglican marriage service the minister speaks of the couple as making a covenant or bargain. A bargain is a two-sided thing. We give something and we get something else in return. In entering into most bargains we want to know, 'Is what I'm getting worth what I'm giving up? Is this transaction worth the price I'm paying for it?' But the Biblical view of marriage is that we should covenant to *be* a bargain, rather than to get one. And that is something that just doesn't come naturally!

If we are willing to try to put giving before receiving in our marriage, we can certainly expect God's help as we pray about the situation and our rôle within it. We've already seen that the only person that we can change, with God's help, is ourselves — so perhaps our most effective prayer will be:

> 'Lord, change me so that I can be the loving partner that you want me to be. Show me what I have to do so that my loved one's need for security and significance is met more fully. Rather than demanding anything in return, I'll trust you to meet my needs.'

That may sound like a very risky prayer to pray, but as Helen Keller said, 'Life is an exciting business and most exciting when it is lived for others.' If that is true, marriage and family living should be pretty exciting, for here, as nowhere else, we have the opportunity to live for others all the way down the line! But how do we do it in practice?

What do you want from me?

Has it ever struck you that we can spend years trying to fulfil expectations and requirements that we *think* other people have for us, only to discover that these expectations exist only in our imagination? On the other hand, we may be disappointing them by failing to fulfil hopes that they *do* have of us, because we don't know what they are.

So far we have thought what *we* might be looking

for within marriage, but if we are choosing to *be* a bargain, our first concern will have to be for our partner's needs. The problem is that it is often difficult to know what those needs are — either because he or she doesn't really know what they are either, or else finds it impossible to put such personal things into words. Of course the best thing to do in this situation is to ask. But if they can't tell us, or don't want to discuss it, we may have to embark on a little detective work.

The outward things are relatively easy to notice and to deal with. We know that we all need to eat and have a home which is a safe place in which to relax and recoup our energies before we go out to face the problems and pressures of the wider world once again. So we can do our part in these practical areas with love and enthusiasm. The inner world of spirit and emotions are more difficult to pinpoint, but there are certain things that we are all silently asking, and words that we all need to hear.

Am I a success in your eyes?

She was beautiful. Even in head and shoulders close-up on the screen, every feature was flawless, but as she gazed into the handsome hero's eyes, she said something that to me, at least, was totally unexpected. 'When I'm with you, I feel good about myself!' When I'm *with you* I feel good...which, by implication at least, suggested that when she was alone she had doubts, even though she was beautiful.

Feeling happy and comfortable with being the person God made me to be is a need we all share, and one that many of us have difficulty in dealing with. One of the ways in which we form a picture of ourselves is from the feedback that we get from other people. So we all need to hear words of appreciation and admiration. Our partner may not have the courage to ask, 'Am I a good husband?' 'Are you satisfied with our life together?' 'Am I a good parent?'. But we all want to hear, 'You're doing a great job' (even if there are a few suggestions for improvement mentioned later on!).

Am I important to you?

Another vital need that we all share is to feel important to someone and an essential part of their lives. We have this need all the time, but when the going gets rough we need reassuring over and over again. When Chrissie and Tracy became Christians, their husbands felt insecure. Suddenly the wives who had depended on them for encouragement and support, had others to turn to — God first and then the new church family. Both men needed to hear that they hadn't lost their importance; that they were still at the centre of their wives' worlds.

'I told Martin over and over again that I didn't know how I managed without him when he was on his long trips,' said Tracy, 'but he didn't seem very convinced. Then I realized why. I caught myself saying that he didn't need to stay in with the boys, because Pat, my friend from church would babysit, while I went to the Bible study group. I thought that I was being helpful; he thought that he wasn't needed any more.'

It is so important that we back up our words with our actions and attitudes. An unkind or unsympathetic reaction can cancel out any number of words, however complimentary. Sue's laughter was close to tears when she said, 'Steve gave me a pretty clear picture of my priority rating when I had an accident in the car last week. When I phoned his office to tell him, his first question was, "How is the car?". His second was, "Are the children O.K.?" Eventually he asked, "How about you?"'

Sometimes, we communicate with one another in a silent code. We quarrel, but what we fall out over, may not be the real point at issue. A couple may argue about the long hours he works or spends at the church, or the fact that the wife spoils the children or sees too much of her Christian friends. But that isn't really the cause of the problem. They may be pinning their resentment on these outward things. But what they are really saying is, 'Are these things or people more important to you than I am?'

When someone feels secure in knowing they are special, loved and valued, he or she can cope with separation, time pressures and the demands of others with comparative ease. But if this sense of being important is missing, they are likely to make more and more frantic efforts to secure it, or else sink down into apathy and despair.

Do you love me?

It is coming up for St Valentine's day as I write this and the shops are full of cards. They express in a thousand different ways — from the frankly vulgar to the purplest prose — what we find so difficult to put into three simple words, 'I love you.' I don't know why many people find it almost as difficult to say, 'I love you' as they do to say, 'I'm sorry', but that does seem to be the case. Perhaps it's a fear of rejection — 'What if he or she doesn't respond?' — or simple embarrassment... 'I'm not one for mushy sentiment!' Maybe words seem too easy or insincere, and action more telling.

Many men prefer action to words. They use words to express ideas, and share information, whereas women use them more easily to reveal feelings and emotion. When a woman says to her husband, 'Do you love me?' and he replies, 'You know that I do — I put up those shelves for you last week, didn't I?' that is quite true. She usually does know. But she has a very real need to hear him *say* it. And she is not alone. Little boys have just as much of a need to know that they are loved and precious, as any little girl, and so do their fathers and grandfathers.

In spite of all the changes in the way we do things, there is still a tendency to think of men as wooers and women as the wooed. Perhaps this is an opportunity to see equality in action! The old saying, 'There is always one who kisses and one who holds the cheek' may be true, but it doesn't always have to be the same one. Both partners need to hear love expressed. 'I love you' in any language and at any age, gives a glow around the heart and is the best tonic available. So let's spell it out in every way and on any occasion that creative caring can devise.

8

God's Beloved Child

KNOWING YOURSELF LOVED AND SECURE

'It sounds wonderful to be able to be so loving and giving,' said Lorna, 'but wouldn't you end up totally drained? After all, I have needs, too! I need to hear Terry say that he loves me a lot more often than he does. It would make me feel great, to know that he thinks I'm Superwoman sometimes — even though I know that I'm not. And that if I walked out of the door and didn't come back, he'd notice *before* he couldn't get into the kitchen for the dirty dishes, or ran out of shirts to wear!'

'When Brian left me,' Rosemary's soft voice trembled on the edge of tears, 'I lost my home, my business partner, and because of that, my income. But the greatest loss of all was my sense of being worth something. I didn't know Jesus then, and so Brian was my mirror. I hadn't realized it until we split up, but his opinion of me had become the way I saw myself.

'His new partner is younger than me, and different in every way. So during those first awful months it seemed as if he hadn't just rejected me, but everything about me. If Brian preferred a cordon bleu cook in jeans, whose sole interest seemed to be catering for parties and having children, then the things that I valued because I thought that they were important to him,

must be worthless. Suddenly my flair for finding business opportunities, my willingness to work all hours
with him; putting off having a family, keeping slim and
dressing elegantly — all the career woman trimmings
— seemed utterly stupid. I could never invest my life in
someone else again. It hurts too much when they let
you down.'

Looking in the right mirror

Humanly speaking, Lorna and Rosemary are quite right.
It is an impossible and draining task to give out constantly without taking in. You can't fill a glass with
water from an empty jug! And while we may rightly
look for loving emotional support from our partner, we
also need to be realistic and realize that we're all imperfect people. We're all liable to fail one another and
there can be a great deal of pain in that — even though
not all of those 'failures' are as devastating and destruc-
tive as the one that Rosemary experienced.

So if we depend on a husband or wife to meet *all*
our needs we're certain to be disappointed because we
are asking for the impossible. As Ruth Graham, the wife
of the world famous evangelist Billy Graham, once
said, 'Allow your husband the privilege of being just a
man. Don't expect him to read your mind and give you
the security, the joy and the peace…that only God can
give.'

Only God can do it

If a couple are preparing for a church wedding, they
are often asked to attend one or more sessions with the
minister who is conducting the service, either alone or
with other couples. At these 'marriage preparation'
groups, they will talk about the meaning and long-term

implications of the vows they are about to undertake. They may discuss 'leaving' and 'cleaving' and giving each other loving support. They may have a look at how conflict can be resolved and how they can communicate with one another more effectively. But there is one vital fact that often seems to be missed out and that is this: *Our individual needs for security and significance can be met fully, only in God.*

Many people with unbelieving partners feel their self-worth being eroded by constant criticism, which is often focused on their supposed foolishness for believing. So rather than depending on one another for those foundational needs to be satisfied, and being disappointed time and again, we each need to put our roots down deeply into a relationship with Jesus. It is only then that we will have the emotional and spiritual resources to be to one another all that we want to be.

You are my beloved...

'We heard at Christmas that another married couple among our friends have separated, and do you know, I really envied them!' Meg screwed up a rather sodden tissue and pulled out a replacement from the box at her side. 'I wish that I had the guts to admit defeat, so that we both have another chance to find happiness. When James said last week that he wasn't sure if he'd ever really been in love with me, and wished that we'd never got married, I thought we'd reached the end of the road. He said that he didn't mean it the next day, but I can't forget it. I feel so unloved.'

There's such tremendous pain in rejection. Although the words may be retracted later and perhaps even denied, they sear our hearts like a branding iron. The trouble is that so many of us are conditioned to expect rejection from childhood onwards. We sense, or are maybe told point blank, that we're not good enough, clever enough, hardworking enough, thin enough, or perhaps even not spiritual enough, to be accepted and loved by the people who are important to us. And so we're constantly seeking for love and reassurance — but we look for it in the wrong places.

Only God loves us without our doing anything to deserve it. Only God knows us through and through, seeing all the ugliness inside that no one else even dreams about — and loves us just the same. Only God was prepared to prove His love by sending Jesus to die on our behalf. Only God says that nothing can destroy His love for us, or separate us from Him. He will never leave us or put another in our place. In that love — and only in that love — can we be totally secure.

Relax in God's love

I remember, way back, when we were going out together and staying at one another's homes for the weekend, Gordon always brought me a cup of tea in bed. I appreciated his gesture of love very much, but it did have one drawback. It meant that I felt that I had to wake up *before* he came in order to comb my hair and make sure that I was looking as presentable as possible! Since I never quite knew what time that was likely to be, I had some rather early wakenings in those early days of our relationship. I hadn't yet learnt to relax in the fact that his love could stand the shock of seeing me first thing in the morning — even if I was tousle-headed and bleary-eyed!

Often, we make the mistake of treating God like a fastidious lover, who has to be kept happy or coaxed back to us. Whereas the Bible tells us that quite the reverse is true. These verses from the Old Testament

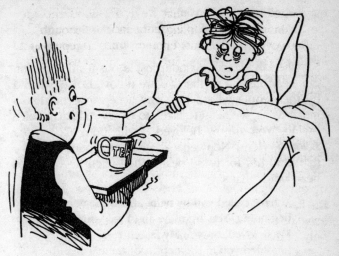

I hadn't yet learnt to relax in the fact that his love could stand the shock of seeing me first thing in the morning.

are just a few of the many that speak of His yearning and beckoning love.

> ...you are my dearest [daughter]
> The child that I love best
> Whenever I mention your name
> I think of you with love,
> My heart goes out to you.   *Jeremiah 31:20*, GNB

> It was I who taught you to walk
> taking you by the arms
> I drew you to me with affection and love
> I picked you up, holding you close to My cheek
> I lifted the yoke from your neck
> and bent down to feed you.   *Hosea 11:3,4*, GNB; NIV

> The mountains and hills may crumble
> But My love for you will never end.
>   *Isaiah 54:10*, GNB

> God has chosen you
> Out of all the peoples on the face of the earth
> To be…His Treasured possession.   *Deuteronomy 7:6*

So when the voices clamour inside our head or within our heart, telling us that we are unloved or unwanted by the people whose love and acceptance means so much to us, we need to listen to God's still small voice saying, 'You are my Beloved.' In his book, *Life of the Beloved*, Henri Nouwen expresses the pulsating love that God has for us so beautifully, when he writes, "I hear words that say:

> "I have called you by name, from the very beginning. You are mine and I am yours. You are My Beloved, on you My favour rests. I have moulded you in the depths of the earth and knitted you together in your mother's womb. I have carved you in the palms of My hands and hidden you in the shadow of My embrace. I look at you with infinite tenderness, and care for you with a care more intimate than that of a mother for her child. I have counted every hair on your head and guided you at every step. Wherever you go, I go with you, and wherever you rest I keep watch. I will give you food that will satisfy all your hunger and drink that will quench all your thirst. I will not hide My face from you. You know Me as your own as I know you as My own. You belong to Me. I am your Father, your Mother, your brother, your sister, your Lover your Spouse…wherever you are I will be. Nothing will ever separate us. We are one."

Is this just one man's idea of how God sees us? No, I'm thankful to say that it isn't. That heartwarming picture of God's love for us is actually a broad paraphrase of verses from the Bible. So we really can relax in the fact that, however falteringly loved or deeply wounded we may have been by others, we have been individually chosen, completely forgiven and unfailingly loved by God Himself.

Receive God's resources

'But I don't *feel* loved.' Meg's tears were flowing in earnest once again. 'I've been taught that God loves me since I was a little girl, but it's something I know in my head, rather than feeling in my heart. If He really loves me like that, why has He let me get my life into such a mess?'

Meg didn't feel the full benefit of God's love for her because she wasn't drawing on the resources available to her. She, like many other Christians, resembled the Texas rancher who used to ride over his land wondering how he was going to pay his bills. Although he had been told that there was oil in the state, and some of his neighbours had arranged for geologists to do test drillings on their land, he couldn't bring himself to believe that such bounty might be available for him. It simply didn't seem worth going to the effort and expense to test it out for himself. That was a great pity because deep down under the surface of his land was a huge oilfield, which, once drilled, could make him a millionaire several times over. He owned the land and the oilfield, but because he wasn't tapping in to what was already his, he was so poor that he was living on government assistance.

Being God's beloved children is certainly something that we *are*; a fact that we need to grasp hold of and accept with our minds. But merely *knowing* it isn't enough. It is also something that we *become* in experience, as we ask the Holy Spirit to make the fact of it so real to us that the way we act is shaped by that knowledge. We need to consciously allow it to underlie and affect everything that we think or say or do.

Sometimes people have great difficulty in accepting God's love for them, and really allowing the Holy Spirit to have free range in their lives. There are many reasons for this, often linked with painful experiences in the past. If this is our situation, we should never feel afraid of asking for help and prayer from wise and mature Christian friends or counsellors. They can help us to see where the problem may lie, and then support and encourage us as we allow the Holy Spirit to heal us and free us to be the people God has made us to be.

Beloved…but still vulnerable

Initially Meg found it difficult to believe that she was beloved, because she felt that if God really loved her so totally, He would surely see to it that her life would be protected from pain. When she began to grasp the reality of God's love no matter what her outward circumstances might be, she felt guilty that she was still hurt by James' attitudes and actions.

'I know I shouldn't be feeling so upset,' she said. 'God's love should be all that I need. But when James says such cutting things I can't seem to stop it getting to me and I still feel devastated. Then I react badly and either feel like lashing out at him or crawling under the nearest stone. It's at those times that I long for someone to hold me. I really sympathize with that little boy who knew he was expected to feel brave in the dark because his mother had told him that Jesus was there with him. And he secretly felt that Jesus was all very well but he wanted "someone with skin on"!'

In the Psalms, King David often speaks about God, and His truth, being like a rock under his feet. God's unfailing love for us is one of those rocks. But have you noticed that when you have scaled a large rock on the beach, perhaps with great difficulty, and you're standing triumphantly on top, it's very easy to take an unwary step to one side, and find yourself flat on your back? As we stand firmly on the fact that we're God's beloved ones, we can so easily do that. Satan loves to take truth and twist it so that it becomes a lie. He wants to lure us into taking a false step, and ending up hurt and ineffective in the spiritual battle. He does it, as he did with Meg, by suggesting to us that if we're *truly* God's Beloved, then:

- We shouldn't have to face pain and difficulty in our lives;
- If others reject us it throws God's love for us into doubt;
- We shouldn't feel pain when others treat us badly;
- If God loves us we don't need other people anyway.

Let us look more closely at those misconceptions:

Life should be all sunshine...
This first one is reasonably easy to recognize and to avoid. We know that because humankind has chosen to live their own sinful and selfish way instead of God's, we all experience pain and difficulty in our lives. Being a Christian doesn't take us out of that situation, but it does offer us the strength to deal with the problems within it, in a different way. When we are tempted to self-pity or despair, we can remind ourselves of the words of Jesus when He said to His disciples: 'In this world you will have trouble. But take heart! I have overcome the world' (*John 16:33*).

If your world doesn't want you...

This second false step is rather easier to stumble into. The habit of looking to others first for approval and finding our self-worth in their opinion of us, dies hard. So when a partner or another Christian appears to reject us, we may *feel* unlovable and it is as if we've got a tape recorder in our minds playing the old message: 'You're a failure...it's obvious you're not really important to them or you wouldn't have been left out...if they reject you why should God be any different...nothing has changed...you're just fooling yourself...you might as well give up.'

> *Sometimes people have great difficulty*
> *in accepting God's love for them,*
> *and really allowing the Holy Spirit*
> *to have free range in their lives.*
> *There are many reasons for this,*
> *often linked with*
> *painful experiences in the past*

Satan is so quick to exploit the old negative thought patterns, that it seems as if he flicks the switch before we're aware of it. When this happens we need to recognize these words for what they are, and then replace those thoughts with a new 'tape' which reminds us of what God says about us.

In *Life of the Beloved* Henri Nouwen reminds us, 'Every time you feel hurt, offended or rejected you have to dare to say to yourself:

> "These feelings, strong as they may be, are not telling me the truth about myself. The truth, even though I cannot feel it right now, is that I am the chosen child of God, precious in His eyes, called

the Beloved from all eternity and held safe in an everlasting embrace."

Writing down some of those Bible verses that I quoted earlier, and saying them over and over to ourselves until we know them by heart, is another way of 'renewing' our minds and thinking in a godly way.

You shouldn't feel like that

The third way in which we may 'fall off the rock' is if we are tempted to feel guilty and unspiritual for having negative emotions. Christians often believe (wrongly) that we 'shouldn't' feel unhappy or hurt, and so we stuff the feelings down below the surface and pretend that all is well when it isn't. We forget that our feelings are God-given, and that it isn't what we feel but how we deal with the emotions within us that is the key issue. Jesus had deep emotions and was angry, sad and disappointed as well as loving, sociable and patient. We forget that we can tell God exactly how we feel and that He understands. The writer to the Hebrews tells us that:

> 'We have a great high priest…Jesus…who has been tempted in every way just as we are — yet was without sin.' *Hebrews 4:15*

And unlike us, Jesus doesn't say, 'Well, I coped, so why can't you?' He listens uncritically and sympathizes — and then reminds us that we can respond in a godly way because His grace is available to us, and that we are secure in His love for us, however we feel.

Who needs intimacy?

The final false step that Satan tries to encourage us to take in this area of appreciating our 'belovedness', is when he suggests to us that if God loves us, we don't or shouldn't need the love of other people. If we feel that we do, then we are failing to really appreciate what God offers us. Satan wants us to forget that God has created us with a capacity for a relationship with Him *and* with others. So if either component is missing, our lives are lopsided and incomplete.

If we fall into this way of thinking we're likely to be tempted to withdraw emotionally and to refuse to allow others to get close to us — or to resist exposing ourselves to hurt or rejection by trying to meet their needs. This is exactly what Satan wants to happen. After all, how can we encourage the fulfilment of our partner's potential, or be an effective and loving member of the church family, if we insist on holding others at arm's length? Getting close to others and being vulnerable and available is a risk — but it is a risk that Jesus took for us, and is one that He asks us to take with others for His sake.

> *Getting close to others and*
> *being vulnerable and available*
> *is a risk — but it is a risk that Jesus*
> *took for us, and is one that He asks us*
> *to take with others for His sake*

In his book entitled *Why am I afraid to tell you who I am?*, John Powell answers his own question when he says, 'If I tell you who I am, you may not like who I am, and that is all I have.'

It is this fear that is the real root cause of our withdrawal. If I let you get close to me and open my heart to you with no holding back, I place myself in your hands and arm you with a weapon of knowledge that you can use to hurt me very deeply.

It seems perfectly reasonable then to be afraid. But this is where our confidence in God and His love for us can take away our fear. We can stand, spiritually naked and vulnerable before Him, and hear Him say:

> 'My child, I know you through and through. Nothing that you, or anyone else can say or do, will ever show Me anything new about you. I know the best and the worst about you and love and accept you just the same. No difficult or testing situation in which you find yourself will take Me by surprise, and your actions or reactions within it will never make you any less precious in my sight. Now go and love that wounded, angry or bitter partner or Christian brother and sister for Me. The way that they respond may hurt you but you need not fear. No wounds that you receive for my sake can destroy you. Stay close to Me because then My love and acceptance surrounds you like an armour of light.'

9

God's Chosen Child

TO BE BLESSED AND TO BE A BLESSING

Eighteen months ago, Gordon and I celebrated our Pearl wedding anniversary — thirty years of loving and living...and sometimes struggling...with one another. Six weeks after that very special day, our older daughter got married. From the moment that the minister pronounced Jo and Stewart to be man and wife, they were as married as we were. But I think that they would have admitted then (and certainly would agree now) that they had a lot of growing into their marriage to do.

I find this a helpful picture of the Christian life. When we first come to faith, we realize for the first time how much God loves us. We marvel and rejoice in the fact that we *are* His Beloved children. But we have a lot of growing *into* the reality of that fact to do. So how does this happen?

There are many ways of describing the process of growing towards Christian maturity, and experiencing the reality of being God's beloved ones. One of the most helpful ones that I have found, is a picture taken from the institution of the communion service. When Jesus celebrated the last Passover Feast with His disciples we read:

> 'He took bread, gave thanks...broke it, and gave it
> to them saying "This is My body given for you; do
> this in remembrance of Me."'   *Luke 22:19*

In his book *Life of the Beloved* Henri Nouwen picks
up those four words to describe this growing process:
Taken, Blessed, Broken and Given. He writes, 'These
words...summarise my life as a Christian because, as a
Christian I am called to become bread for the world:
Bread that is taken, blessed, broken and given.'

You are my Beloved — My chosen child

When our younger daughter was four she was given a
tee-shirt for her birthday. On the front was the logo
'Someone special' and on the back were the words
'Carefully chosen and Completely paid for.' Icilda loved
that tee-shirt and insisted on wearing it long after it was
noticeably too small. I don't think that it was the colour
(deep, though soon to be faded, turquoise) or the 'glit-
ter dust' that sparkled back and front. Young as she was,
she knew that it was great to be special and chosen.

We all inwardly long to be 'Someone special', even
though we might not want to have it emblazoned
across our chest. And this need for significance, to be
'taken' or 'chosen', is the other foundational area of our
lives that God alone can meet in full. Jesus said:

> 'You did not choose me, but I chose you to go and
> bear fruit — fruit that will remain.'   *John 15:16*

Have you ever asked yourself what the point of life
really is? How your existence can have any lasting
impact even within your own small circle? In these days
of computers and data banks can you identify with
Anna Karenina, who at her death was described as
becoming 'a nameless number, on a list that was later

mislaid'? Well the good news is that there is an eternal reason for our being here. God has not only chosen us for ourselves, because He loves us, but He has also chosen us to 'bear fruit — fruit that will remain.'

Chosen...but what have I got to offer?

Many of us have a distinctly wobbly sense of self-worth. This is something that God gradually deals with as we grow to appreciate the reality and practicality of His love for us. Looking at ourselves, we may not see much potential for fruit bearing, but just as the seed has everything it needs within it to produce the flower or fruit that it was created to produce, so it is with us. It's all there, just waiting for the Holy Spirit to be released into our lives, and for us to be obedient to His prompting.

Chosen...to bear fruit in my circumstances?

So you feel that you're in a hard and barren place — one in which it's unreasonable to expect anything worthwhile to grow? God hasn't promised to put us in situations where we'll always feel comfortable or in control. He is principally concerned that our lives are fruitful. And in the same way that many plants have to be staked and pruned in order to bear a better crop, so it is with us. The most desirable fruit often grows in unlikely places.

If we have a marriage partner who doesn't share our faith, it's especially easy to feel limited and constrained in our 'fruit bearing' by our circumstances. We need not be. God knows the things that form boundaries in our lives. He isn't limited by them. The Psalmist says:

> **'He grants peace to your borders and satisfies you with the finest of wheat.'**   *Psalm 147:14*

So we don't have to chafe at and struggle with those things that we see as restrictions. When we accept them as part of God's will for us, He promises peace, and the finest of wheat — not some sub-standard straw — within them.

Chosen...to bear fruit in our attitudes and actions

As the Holy Spirit begins His work in us, the first harvest that God looks for is fruit of character. In his letter to the Ephesian Christians, Paul describes the way that they used to live and behave as the fruitlessness of darkness, and contrasts that with the fruit of the light — goodness, truth and righteousness. Writing to the church in Galatia he expands this further as he says:

> 'The fruit of the Spirit is love, joy, peace, patience, kindness, goodness, faithfulness, gentleness and self control.'
>
> *Galatians 5:20*

These qualities of character describe Jesus. As His life develops within us, we too can begin to demonstrate them, regardless of the outer circumstances. Indeed, although it may seem brutal to say so, it is often the problems that we wrestle with that act as manure to produce a bumper crop!

---

*And in the same way that
many plants have to be staked and
pruned in order to bear a better crop,
so it is with us. The most desirable
fruit often grows in unlikely places.*

This new life in the Spirit is not to do with having our head in the clouds. Our feet are very much on the ground, and our opportunities for growth are present in our everyday lives.

'I never knew that I had a temper until I had this lot to look after,' said Sally, ruefully looking at her three-year-old twins and her daughter who was a year older. 'If I didn't keep praying for patience, I'd probably murder the lot of them on a rainy day like today!'

'But I want to do more for God than simply look after my family,' said Jenny. 'Something big; something significant; something that really makes a difference in His Kingdom'.

Like Jenny, many of us think of bearing fruit for God as being solely the things that we achieve *for* Him. But what we are and what we do go hand in hand. Our actions have to flow out of our attitudes. Having said that, God does have things for us to do, especially designed and fitted to our circumstances and talents. Like those wonderful creations on the children's TV programme, *Blue Peter*, He has even prepared them for us ahead of time, for the book of Ephesians tells us:

> **'We are God's workmanship, created in Christ Jesus to do good works which God prepared in advance for us to do.'**   *Ephesians 2:10*

Our part in the procedure is to ask God what these 'good works' are that we (not any other Christians) should be doing and then, as He leads us into them, to get on with the job.

Chosen...to bear fruit by our influence:

'Influence other people for God — *me*?' Lorna pulled a disbelieving face. 'Terry makes a terrible fuss if I want to offer to help with anything at church, my neighbours are all out at work, and so apart from going down to the school, I never see anyone *to* influence. I might as well be in prison — then at least I'd have the other prisoners and the warders to talk to!'

It is very easy to feel cut off from the 'real' world if we are at the stage of life when home-making and children fill most of our day. But Lorna was underestimating her potential. First of all, she took God's presence into her home — she was His sole representative to her husband and children so her influence there was enormous and crucial. Then she was a very active member of the Parent Teacher Association in the primary school that her children attended. She helped in the classroom twice a week, encouraging a small group of children who were struggling with reading, and making life easier for at least two of the teachers. At her suggestion, her church had donated £250.00 worth of carefully selected Christian books for the Religious Education part of the National Curriculum. And the friendships that she struck up at the school gate gave a number of young mothers their only contact with someone who knew Jesus as a living day to day reality. She rarely had the opportunity to speak about Him, but His presence was felt, everywhere she went.

Chosen...with others
Most of us can remember uncomfortable moments in games lessons at school when teams were being chosen. It was all very well if you were one of the 'captains' and doing the choosing, but many old scores could be settled by leaving your 'enemies' till last. The humiliation of not being wanted is terrifying.

I'm thankful to say that in God's Kingdom the selection process is not the same as in the world. In daily life, if ten people are applying for a job, one is chosen and filled with joy, but the other nine are bitterly disappointed. With God it is different. He holds out His hand to choose each one of us. All are chosen in the sense that they are invited to come. But not all walk over to join His team. Many walk away, unwilling to give up their life to gain His. That is their decision, and God gives them the freedom to make it. Those of us who do respond to His invitation however, can celebrate and be thankful, without feeling guilty or having our joy dimmed by the disappointment of others at being left out.

Chosen...in the church

Recognizing that God's choosing includes us all cuts out any sense of competition and comparison. There is a place for everyone — a unique and special place. So I don't have to struggle to be more holy than you, to serve more faithfully than you, or to love God more than you, in order to win God's favour. Your behaviour in these and many other areas may be a spur to my spiritual zeal, and a challenge to my commitment. But we are both 'family', part of the same team, and unfailingly loved and valued by a Father who has no favourites. And this applies as much to those whom I see as unspiritual, or find irritating or difficult to understand, as it does to those who inspire, love and support me.

This is particularly important for those who are 'single' Christians within the church. God loves me and has chosen me for being me. My 'Belovedness' is in no way increased by whether I have a believing partner, children who are leading lights in the youth group, a role in the church that everyone notices, or a pewful of people that I have lead to Christ. It isn't decreased if I have none of these things. I can rejoice in my 'chosenness' for myself, affirm and enjoy it in other people, and thank God for it on a daily basis.

You are my Beloved — blessed without limit:

When we were having tea with an elderly couple recently, our hostess turned to her husband and said, 'George dear, will you say a blessing for the food before we begin? He held out his hands over the table, blessed the food, and thanked God for his provision. This is what Jesus did at the Last Supper. He took the bread into His hands and thanked God for it and all that it represented.

Thankfulness is one meaning of the word blessing. When we recognize and accept that we're God's blessed ones, we understand in a new way that all that happens in our lives can only occur if it is part of His plan for us. All that we have and are comes from God and so we can receive it from Him with thanksgiving.

The other major definition of 'blessing' that my dictionary gives is 'to make happy; to be the recipient of divine favour.' The Bible is full of promises of God's favour resting upon us, and bringing us lasting happiness if we will only walk in His ways. In the New Testament Paul speaks of God's blessing in an outpouring of praise when he says:

> **Praise be to the God and Father of our Lord Jesus Christ, who has blessed us in the heavenly realms with every spiritual blessing in Christ.** *Ephesians 1:3*

What are these 'spiritual blessings'? Some we've already thought about. We've been chosen since the beginning of time. Freely forgiven because of what Jesus has done. His will has been made known to us — in part, if not in the whole. The Holy Spirit has been given to us, both to assure us that we truly are God's children, and also so that we have the power to live lives that are pleasing to God and that bring Him honour and glory.

Enjoying God's blessing

How does the assurance that God is 'for us', heaping blessings on us and longing to bless us more, affect the way we live as God's Beloved?

First of all, it gives us confidence, acting as a corrective to our view of God. Many of us have grown up with the notion that God is some sort of super-strict headmaster, laying down rules and then vengefully watching to catch us out when we fail. So that although we give lip service to the fact that He is a loving Father, in the depths of our heart we tend to regard Him as if He is against us rather than on our side.

Secondly, it gives us encouragement. When Jesus was baptized by John, He and those around Him heard an audible voice saying:

> 'You are My Son, whom I love; with You I am well pleased' (Mark 1:11).

God must have known that in His humanity, Jesus would need that clear-cut assurance to carry Him through the opposition, difficulties and dangers ahead. And if He needed reassurance and encouragement, we certainly do! God may not give us the privilege of hearing an audible voice, but we can meditate on the Bible verses that speak of God's love for us, and hear His voice speaking deep within us. And as we live day by day, remembering that God's intention is to bless us, we become increasingly aware of the resources that are at our disposal. It's like having a spiritual bank account that we can draw on at any time, even, or perhaps especially, when we're not feeling on top of the world spiritually.

The third way in which an awareness of being God's blessed ones makes a tangible difference to us is that it helps to lift us above our circumstances. The Bible says that the world is under a curse because of sin, and it is certainly very easy to feel cursed rather than blessed. Listen to the conversations that you hear on the bus, at the supermarket or in the office, or think about the news that you read in the paper or see on television. So much centres on the negative and the downright gloomy! But if, in the midst of fractious families, financial difficulties or the dark days of spiritual oppression, we can focus our mind on God's blessings we will find that our whole outlook changes. I used to sing the chorus in Sunday School which said:

> **When upon life's billows you are tempest tossed,**
> **When you are discouraged, thinking all is lost,**
> **Count your many blessings, name them one by one,**
> **And it will amaze you what the Lord has done.**

It may sound rather old-fashioned, but it contains a great deal of truth. So next time you wake up feeling as if your spirit is weighed down, try listing your blessings, one by one. I guarantee that it will transform your day!

Claiming God's blessing

'Those that ask, don't get!' Did you have that said to you as a child, or perhaps say it to your own children? The idea behind it is fair enough — we don't want our children to grow up selfish and grasping. But the spiritual life is different. To take an example from the Old Testament: when Jacob was wrestling with the angel sent from God (you can read the full story in Genesis 32) he clung on tenaciously saying, 'I will not let you go unless you bless me.' God honoured him for his determination and 'blessed him there.'

Jabez is another Old Testament man who was bold

enough to ask God for a big blessing. He must have had a difficult start in life because we read:

> His mother named him Jabez because she had
> such a hard time at his birth. [Jabez means
> Distress] But undeterred he prayed, 'Oh that you
> would wonderfully bless me and help me in my
> work; please be with me in all that I do, and keep
> me from all evil and disaster.' And God granted
> him his request.   *I Chronicles 4:9*, Living Bible

Did you notice that God gave him what he asked for? If we're not enjoying or experiencing God's blessing, perhaps it is because, unlike Jabez and Jacob, we've never asked. The Bible tells us that if what we are asking for is something that will honour and glorify God, then we can ask for it, and go on asking, with confidence. And that must surely include being united in faith with the one we love and share our life with.

10

God's Fruitful Child

BEARING FRUIT IN DIFFICULT CIRCUMSTANCES

Sue came to the prayer corner after the morning service with tears streaming down her face. 'I doubt if I'll be able to keep going much longer,' she wept. 'We had such a row before I came to church this morning because Steve suddenly decided that we were all going to the car boot sale. He knew that I was due to play my guitar for Sunday Gang. We'd talked about it before I committed myself to do it — only once a month — and he'd agreed. I'd even put it on the kitchen calendar so he had no excuse for saying that he hadn't realized that it was today. We were both so angry, the whole thing got completely out of hand. I was half expecting him to say that it was either him or Jesus and I was muttering under my breath "Don't push me too far Steve. If you try to make me choose, you may not be the one who'll come out the winner!"'

Fruit in a hostile climate

After Sue and I had prayed together, I looked at some of the other people who had come forward to lay their distress before God. A young mother who had recently had an operation for breast cancer was listening to an elderly widow. A middle-aged father of four, who had just been made redundant for the second time, was sitting with head bowed while his friend simply stood beside him, a comforting hand on his shoulder. A student from one of our local colleges knelt silently in the corner. The sense of pain in that quiet place was almost tangible.

Does it surprise you that Christians who are both chosen and blessed by God are also broken? Perhaps it does, because like Meg, many of us secretly believe that if God *really* loves us and has chosen us to accomplish great things for Him, He surely isn't going to allow life to be difficult for us. In fact sometimes we experience more pain over the fact that we *have* the trial than actually results from the problem itself!

When this happens, it shows that our trust in God has less effect in our lives than the influence of our culture, where weakness, pain and brokenness are seen as highly undesirable experiences. Both those of us who are Christians and those who aren't tend to try to avoid them at all costs, or, if they can't be avoided, push them down under the surface of our lives and ignore them as far as possible.

And yet we shouldn't be surprised when difficulties arise. The Bible gives us many pictures of things being broken so that they can be put together again. There is the potter remaking the pot that is misshapen; the blacksmith who forges a weapon in the heat of the flame, and the jeweller refining gold and silver. The aim of all this activity is to produce something more pure, more useful and more suited for what it is to be used for.

Over and over again the New Testament writers warn us that pressure is to be expected, and assure us that our faith can flourish in the midst of suffering and testing. Jesus Himself warned us that we shouldn't

expect an easier life than He had. He told the first
disciples:

> No pupil is greater than his teacher; no slave is
> greater than his master. So a pupil should be
> satisfied to become like His teacher, and a slave
> like his master. If the head of the family is called
> Beelzebub, the members of the family will be
> called even worse names.   *Matthew 10:24, 25*

Jesus experienced it all. He knew emotional pain
and great loneliness. His family misunderstood His
motives and tried to put a stop to His ministry. His
heart was torn when His closest friends betrayed Him,
ran away when He was arrested and finally denied
even knowing Him when He was on trial for His life.
He knew little of physical comfort throughout His lifetime, and in His death endured the indescribable tor-
ture of crucifixion. He experienced spiritual darkness of
a kind that we can't begin to imagine as He carried the
sins of the whole world on His shoulders. And at that
rock-bottom point even God the Father turned His back
on Him.

Many people think the Christian faith is a refuge or
a crutch for those who can't cope with life's difficulties
on their own. But this is only half the story. We have
only got to look around us to see the truth of the novel-
ist Ernest Hemingway's observation: 'Life breaks us all.
But some are made strong at the broken places.'
Christians, like the rest of humanity, may be broken
people but they know where to go to get themselves,
not just mended but, reinforced!' And the key to trans-
forming the situation is to ask the right question. Not,
'Why is that happening to me?' but 'What fruit is God
wanting to produce in my life through this? How will

He make me strong at the very place where I'm naturally most likely to give way?'

'Fruit that will last'

Two very important types of 'fruit' that God wants to produce in our lives are faith and perseverance. In his New Testament letter, James goes as far as to say that we should welcome difficulties for that very reason. He writes:

> Consider it pure joy, my brothers, whenever you face trials of many kinds, because you know that the testing of your faith develops perseverance. Perseverance must finish its work so that you may be mature and complete, not lacking anything.
>
> *James 1:2-4*

Does this mean that we have to go round with a plastic smile, pretending that we're happy to suffer? No! We don't go out looking for trouble so that we can endure suffering for its own sake. But we can be positive about such times when they come if we understand that although the trial itself has no power to produce fruit in our lives, our faith and perseverance in the midst of it will. That is God's 'superglue' which will make us so 'strong at the broken places' that the very thing we feared can become the means of blessing to ourselves and to others.

Enduring the Heat

When we had our first family holiday in France, our campsite was on a south-facing scrub-covered hillside above a vineyard. It was August and there was precious little shade for us, but down among the vines the heat absolutely shimmered. The farmer chugged up and down on his little tractor, weeding, watering, spraying and constantly checking on the grapes which would soon be ready for harvest. The heat didn't appear to bother him one bit. Quite the reverse. He would have been very anxious if the clouds had gathered and given what to us would have been welcome coolness. In order to ripen, grapes need a certain number of hours when the sun is shining and the temperature is in the high 80s or low 90s Fahrenheit, and so his comfort was unimportant. The harvest was his only concern.

Monsieur Dessin, our French farmer, could endure the heat cheerfully because there was something valuable to be gained by doing so. The Bible tells us that Jesus was able to endure the agony of the cross because of the 'joy set before Him'. Unlikely as it may seem at times, we too can see something beautiful emerge from our brokenness, especially if we are willing to take certain practical steps to help ourselves and then trust God to do His part.

Recognize the season what is at stake

When we first come to faith, or experience a fresh touch from God, it's like the springtime. Everything is exciting and the Holy Spirit's work in our lives is fresh and full of potential. Even if our partner is not over-excited by the decision we've made, he or she may be prepared to give us the benefit of the doubt. There may well be a honeymoon period while we both take stock and see what difference this change will make.

And then the summer comes, and with it opposition and discouragement if our partner shows no inclination to share the faith we've found to be so life-changing. In Britain the summer is a time to be welcomed and looked forward to. Sunshine is a precious commodity in our climate. But in countries where grapes are usually grown, the heat is both a friend and a potential enemy. It ripens the fruit, certainly, but it also threatens to suck every ounce of moisture out of the soil. It enables weeds to germinate and flourish, and insects to reproduce in their thousands. The farmer has to be constantly at work or the harvest will be meagre at best, or perhaps lost altogether.

One of the things that we noticed about Monsieur Dessin was that he worked steadily in the vineyard, but he focused on the essential tasks. It was fairly obvious that in the autumn he would need to repair some of the stone walls that surrounded his vines. But in the summer he hadn't got time for that. Watering, weeding and spraying were the priorities of the moment, and he stuck to them. We also noticed that although he worked very hard, he wasn't averse to taking a nap in the heat of the day.

The summer season in our spiritual lives is just like that. Satan uses our circumstances to put pressure on us, sucking up our spiritual energy like water from the ground, sowing the weeds of worry and fear, and sending the buzzing and biting 'insects' of doubt and disappointment in clouds. And like Monsieur Dessin, at this season we need to focus on the essentials, however many other things seem to be crying out for our attention.

Just before He died, Jesus talked to His twelve closest disciples at some length about a vineyard.

> 'I am the vine;' He said, 'you are the branches. If a man remains in Me and I in him, he will bear much fruit; apart from Me you can do nothing'
> (*John 15:15*).

Remaining 'in the vine' — firmly attached to Jesus — is the first and most important thing that we have to do.

If His life and power is constantly flowing through us, then we *will* produce fruit, no matter how hostile the environment in which we find ourselves. In order to 'remain in Him' we need to make time to stay in touch, listening to what He has to say to us, and responding to His guidance. Although praying and reading the Bible may be the last thing that we feel like doing, when the sun of persecution or opposition is burning down on us, it is so important that we do so. Even though the way we do it and the time we have to spend may be very different from what we've done before.

Remaining 'in the vine' — firmly attached to Jesus — is the first and most important thing that we have to do

---

Release the problems to God

When Ginny's husband had a breakdown, losing his faith, his job, and because of that, their home, Ginny felt too exhausted to concentrate on her normal pattern of devotions. 'I simply read a verse from the Bible — or sometimes even a hymn,' she said, 'and then I imagined putting all the things that I was worried about — including Gerald — into a basket. I said to God, "You know what's in here — please take it" and then He and I just sat there together. I don't often use that way of praying now that things are more normal in our lives,' she continued, 'but I'm glad that I had that experience. I learned more about resting in God and trusting Him then than I did when I was doing detailed Bible study and praying for lots of people at great length.'

Another important way to keep the sap flowing is meeting with other Christians to worship God and to be taught about Him. But when there is friction at home about our faith, sometimes it is right to give Sunday services a slightly lower profile for a while. After Sue fell out with Steve about the car boot sale, the leader of the music group suggested that she should be released from any regular commitment to play her guitar that summer. 'If you're here we'll use you,' he said, 'but we're not too short of guitarists at the moment, so we can afford to be flexible.'

At first Sue was very reluctant to agree to this. She liked playing the guitar for the children in Sunday Gang; it made her feel valued and as if she belonged to the church. It also gave her a good reason to insist on being there on a regular basis! 'I missed seeing my friends too,' she said, 'and I felt I was being deprived of regular teaching. But very reluctantly I told God that if that was what He wanted I'd do it, and trust Him to see that I didn't miss out.'

'Once Steve realized that I was giving him and the children a higher priority than getting to church every Sunday morning, he stopped hassling me. And God did meet my needs. One of my friends from church offered to baby-sit so that I could get to the mid-week Bible study. This was held on a night when Steve was at night school so I'd never been able to go before. I found that studying the Bible with other people was just as helpful as lots of sermons I've heard! I also discovered that there was a Christian Union at the hospital where I work, and I was able to rearrange my lunch hour so that I could get along to their worship service in the Chapel every couple of weeks. And once the winter came, Steve started playing hockey again, so he didn't mind if I took the children to church as long as we went along to the home matches sometimes.'

Respond to the Holy Spirit

One of the ways in which the Holy Spirit is described in the Bible is 'living water'. The vineyard in summer certainly needs plenty of that. In the small vineyard that we overlooked while camping twenty years ago, watering was a fairly simple operation, from a barrel on the back of a tractor! But in larger scale, more commercial operations today, there is often an underground irrigation system, which delivers the water well under the surface of the field, and directly to the roots. This has obvious advantages, but it also has the potential for problems if leaves, earth, or roots block the pipes. The vine may be starved of water for some time before the farmer is aware of the fact, and when the vine begins to show signs of drying out, it is sometimes too late to revive it.

If we are to stay green and productive in a hostile climate, we need the Holy Spirit to flow unchecked in our lives. The most basic need for our water pipe of course, is that it should be firmly connected to the source of supply, and the mains system should be turned on. But many of us are rather wary of this in case we get 'flooded out'! We're ready to let the Holy Spirit have control of one small part of our life — but prefer to keep the rest very firmly in our own hands…just in case. God spoke to Clare about this when she was at the swimming pool with her children.

'I was sitting by this huge fountain,' she said, 'which looks pretty, but is really there to keep the water circulating through the filtration system. The water never stops flowing. Beside it is one of those small drinking fountains, and my little boy was pressing the foot pedal so that he could have a drink. He didn't want the water to splash his face, so he kept taking his foot off the pedal before the jet had bounced up high enough for him to catch it in his mouth. As I watched him, God spoke to me so clearly.

"'Your attitude to My Spirit is like Mark's with the drinking fountain,' He said. "I want you to experience the constant powerful flow of the ornamental fountain which keeps the whole system clean and usable. But you are making do with the small jet that the drinking fountain offers, because you think that you can control it. When are you going to take your foot off the pedal and allow Me to direct the flow? Only in that way will your thirst be satisfied.'"

Once the source of supply is turned on, and the water is flowing through the pipes, the only thing that can interfere with its effectiveness is blockages in the system. Anger and bitterness are two very solid plugs which can form when we are having a difficult time at home, and perhaps feel misunderstood or unsupported in the church.

When Debbie became a Christian she threw herself into her new life with great enthusiasm. 'I ran the Mums and Toddlers Club, and started a new system for the catering in the church,' she said. 'Soon every event that needed food provided in the church was my responsibility. I was happy to do it; it had been my job before I got married. I was on the PCC and the church's Building Committee — to have my say about the new kitchen and the creche facilities, and I loved it all. Bill was hardly ever at home and the children were almost grown up — there didn't seem to be any reason not to be involved.

'Then my youngest son started experimenting with drugs and I heard whispers that Bill was seeing his sec-

retary out of business hours. I was so *angry*. I was angry with God for letting me down — as I saw it — when I was working so hard for Him. I was angry with Colin for allowing himself to get dragged in to the drugs and party scene, and I was furious with Bill.

'Faced with that situation I made a conscious decision to put my marriage and family first and so I cut down drastically on my church commitments. And guess what happened? The vicar felt let down and said so, and suddenly I wasn't one of the inner circle any more. I felt really bitter about that. Then God seemed miles away and my interest in spiritual things began to wane — my prayers just seemed to bounce off the ceiling.

'Thankfully one of my friends was sensitive enough to see what was happening. I met her regularly to pray about the whole situation, and I began to see how this anger and bitterness was destroying me. Very slowly I was able to let it go, and come to God for His forgiveness. I came out of that experience a very different person.'

Rest in God's love

There is a time for everything, and a season for every activity under heaven,' writes the Teacher in the book of Ecclesiastes. Doing our part to see that the promise of spring flourishes and develops into the harvest of autumn will be quite a challenge. We may need to be inventive in the heat of the spiritual 'summer season', finding fresh ways of drawing nourishment from the Vine. We will have to keep a vigilant eye on the weeds that may grow up, or the blockages that can stem the flow of the Spirit. But we also need to know when to 'step in to the shade,' and leave the rest to God.

> *Once the source of supply is turned on, and the water is flowing through the pipes, the only thing that can interfere with its effectiveness is blockages in the system*

There is our part and God's part in every spiritual battle, and it's important to detect the right time to step out of the way and let God do what we can't. There are a number of occasions in the Bible where the people were told to, 'Stand still and see what God will do,' or to 'wait'. In those times of enforced inactivity, we're not failing if we simply rest in Him, and experience His healing and restoring touch. Jesus said that He had come to:

> Bind up the broken hearted, to proclaim freedom
> for the captives and release for the prisoners…to
> comfort all who mourn and…grieve — to bestow
> on them a crown of beauty instead of ashes, the
> oil of gladness instead of mourning, and a garment
> of praise instead of a spirit of despair

and that is true right the way through our walk with
Him, and not just at the beginning.

Reaping the harvest

The farmer judges when the grapes are ready to be
picked, by assessing their sweetness and their softness.
And it is the same with us. God works within us to
bring about the brokenness, humility and dependence
on Himself which will smooth the rough corners of our
personality. He softens our heart with gentleness and
sweetens it with His overflowing love and kindness.

Some of us may be afraid that if God does that in us,
we'll be taken advantage of and trampled under foot by
those who see gentleness and sweetness of spirit as
weakness. But as Wayne Jacobsen observes in his
book, *The Vineyard*:

> Softness is not weakness; in God's kingdom it is
> the measure of strength. The disciples didn't
> understand this fact, even after walking with Jesus
> a few years. James and John wanted to call down
> fire from heaven when people in a Samaritan
> village wouldn't extend hospitality to Him. They
> were ready to usher in His promise the world's
> way. 'We'll show them who's boss.'
>   But as an old man, John shows us that being
> with Jesus for all those years had finally borne
> fruit when he writes, 'We should love one
> another…we ought to lay down our lives for our

brothers...dear children, let us not love with
words or tongue, but with actions and in truth.'

And that is the Father's ultimate ambition for all of us.
He chooses us, blesses us, breaks down our sinful attitudes so that He can mould us into His likeness, and
then gives us to a weary and lost generation to serve
them in His name.

11

God's Serving Child

LOVE IN ACTION

'It's your turn to do the washing up!'
   'No it's not. I did it after breakfast!'
   'Breakfast doesn't count. This is the dirty washing up, and I'm not doing it!'

Do you ever have conversations like that in your house? We certainly did when our children were all living at home, and washing up after the evening meal meant a mountain of dishes for seven or eight people. That is why we had a rota pinned firmly to the kitchen door!

I don't know whether the disciples had a rota deciding who would be responsible for providing the evening meal for the twelve of them — probably not since they moved from town to town and were often invited into peoples' homes, as was customary in that culture. But on the night before His death Jesus wanted to be alone with His particular friends. So He sent Peter and John ahead of Him into Jerusalem to find a room, and to prepare for the Passover meal.

Love in Action

From what we read in the Gospels, they did a pretty good job. The lamb and bitter herbs were cooked to a turn. The unleavened bread and the wine were on the table. There was water, a basin and at least one towel on the side. But one thing was missing. No one had volunteered to do the ritual footwashing. This was the slave's job, and the services of a slave appear not to have come with the offer of the upper room. It must have been rather embarrassing. The roads in Palestine were dusty, and sandalled feet got hot and dirty. Reclining round a low table meant that your feet were extremely close to your neighbour's nose — and yet still no one made a move. Then Jesus got up, stripped off His robe, tied a towel round His waist and washed their feet.

This incident is often explained as the ultimate example of humility. But in his Gospel, John interprets it differently. He said that Jesus did it to show the disciples the full extent of His love. By washing their feet, He was showing them that they had no need — physical or spiritual — which was beneath His dignity to meet or outside the scope of His love to notice. And this is the quality of love He asks them — and us — to show to one another. 'Love each other.' Three times He repeated it. The supreme fruit of God's work in our lives is this all-prevailing, self-sacrificing love, and this is what He wants us to give to others in His name.

We have spent a considerable part of the last few chapters reflecting on the fact that we are God's Beloved children. But love is a two-way affair. And hard as it may be for us to grasp, God is a lover who longs for us to respond to Him in love. Peter had failed dismally when his love had been put to the test, but when Jesus met him on the shores of the lake (recorded in John, chapter 21), it wasn't an apology He asked for, but an assurance from Peter that His love for him was returned. More than that, Jesus challenged him to back up what he said, by what he did.

> 'Simon,' said Jesus, 'do you truly love Me?'
> He answered, 'Yes, Lord, you know that I love you.'
> Jesus said, 'Take care of my sheep.'

Peter had a choice. He could have argued that he could no longer trust himself or made a hundred other excuses. He could have said no, but we know from his later behaviour that he said 'Yes' with all his heart.

The same challenge faces us. We often sing of our love for God and our thankfulness to Him for all that He has done for us. We may tell God how much we love Him in our private prayers. Words are easily said. But the outworking of those words has to be the same for us as it was for the first disciples:

> 'love one another...lay down your life...love in actions and in truth.'

We have the option to say 'Yes' or 'No' but we need to realise that the answer we give will have a practical effect on our lives. So if we say, 'Yes, Lord,' how is it going to work out in practice, especially if we have a partner who doesn't share our commitment to Jesus?

Fruitful for a purpose

Fruit is grown for a reason. A farmer doesn't leave his grapes on the vine when they are ripe, so that he can pop out and admire them from time to time. If he did they would wither and spoil. They are cut and used with joy. Fruit from plants and trees has two possible uses — it supplies food for nourishment, and seed to be sown. And this is the function of the fruit of God's working in our life. It grows so that we are more able to be a blessing: nourishing and strengthening our partner, meeting his or her needs, and encouraging growth towards wholeness in every way we can.

We are also to be like seeds: people that God can use to draw others into His Kingdom. The Bible tells us that people who don't know God can't see or understand Him in spiritual terms, so He needs to demonstrate Himself in people. How will they know about His patient love, if we don't love them? How will they experience His kindness and forgiveness unless we are kind and forgiving? Jesus is the supreme example of God's life lived out in human form, but now we are His body; His hands and feet.

What's in it for me?

We have already thought about covenanting with God to be a 'bargain', rather than expecting to receive a bargain, within marriage, but many of us find it difficult to see how we could do that if our partner isn't going to respond in the same way. 'You can't really expect one half of a marriage partnership to lay down his or her life for the other, unless they are both prepared to do it,' argued Hilary. 'Surely the Christian partner would get trampled under foot!'

Hilary's reaction reflects the feelings of many. In today's anti-authority 'Do what feels right for you' society we've become very wary of putting ourselves at the mercy of anyone else, even in the best of situations. And if by doing so, we think that we're likely to be exploited or taken advantage of, then that rules it right out! We seem to have forgotten that Jesus said, 'Go the extra mile —for those who treat you badly. Give your coat as well as your cloak — to your enemies.' Footwashing in the middle of the 1990's is distinctly out of fashion.

This self-protection is a very understandable reaction, but it does cause us some problems when we read in Paul's letter to the Ephesians:

> Honour Christ by submitting to each other. You wives must submit to your husband's leadership in the same way you submit to the Lord…And you husbands, show the same kind of love to your wives as Christ showed to the church when He died for her…That is how husbands should treat their wives, loving them as part of themselves…and the wife must see to it that she deeply respects her husband.
>
> From *Ephesians 5:21 – 33*, Living Bible

What does it mean to submit to one another? Does it mean that there is no longer any authority or leadership to be exercised between Christians? Can we dismiss the idea of submission within marriage, by saying that it obviously came out of the apostles' understanding of the culture of the time, when women were little more than chattels anyway? Or is it perhaps only applicable to a marriage between Christians, who will each carry out their side of the equation with loving fairness? Does being married to someone who doesn't share our faith let us off the hook?

Some people would argue that the Bible gives us grounds for believing all these things. Certainly in the society of the New Testament times women weren't highly regarded. But Jesus didn't live according to the norms of his society. He spoke to women in public, included them among His travelling companions, healed them and taught them. What's more, He entrusted them with being the first witnesses to His resurrection at a time when a woman wasn't considered capable of being a reliable witness in a court of law. So

He obviously valued women, and wasn't afraid to demonstrate that fact. And His disciples would have been well aware of it.

It's true that what Paul wrote about 'submitting to one another' and 'wives submitting to your husband as to the Lord' follows the instruction to the Ephesian church to 'be filled with the Spirit'. So this could be understood as an instruction for relationships between Christians *only*. On the other hand it could be read as an instruction to a wife to submit to her husband — Christian or otherwise — in the same way as she would submit to Jesus, or to do it for His sake. And certainly when the apostle Peter was writing about the same subject in his epistle (1 Peter 3:1) he specifically referred it to women whose husbands were unbelievers. So how can we sort out what that means for us, in practical terms, at the end of the twentieth century?

The role of women in the church is a huge subject, which we haven't the space to explore in detail here. But as far as I can see, the balance of Biblical argument is that men and women are absolutely equal in God's sight. Both have the privilege of being heirs of His Kingdom; both are those who are recipients of His gifts and channels of His power. But within marriage there is a difference in their roles and responsibilities. Paul isn't simply saying, 'this is the way you are to treat each other as Christ's followers,' or even 'if you behave in this way you will find that your partner responds,' but, 'In marriage this is God's standard for husbands...and for wives.'

What Paul seems to be doing is calling both to live a life of love and submission to one another; both are being asked to give 100%, whether or not their partner shares their faith or their attitude to marriage. It's the way in which this loving consideration and support works out in practice, for the husband and for the wife, that is different.

Christian husbands — model yourself on Jesus!

I imagine that what Paul said to women, probably didn't cause many ripples among them initially, because it was what they would have expected to hear. As we've already seen, the culture of the time was one of male authority and female submission. But what would have set tongues wagging, and been totally revolutionary, was the idea of the 'new model husband' to whom she was being asked to submit! Someone who put her needs and interests first. Not a common experience in first century A.D!

It must have been a considerable shock, too, for the Christian husband, who is now asked to put aside his own desires in order to love his wife into wholeness. And he is to do this, whether or not she shares his faith, or lovingly lays down her life for him in response. True, as he does so, he is also asked to accept the job of being the one with whom the buck ultimately stops. But even this isn't allowed to give him any excuse for having a 'King complex'! Before he gets any big ideas, Paul is quick to point out that a man's attitude to his wife should be just the same as that of Jesus to his bride the church, and think what that is like! Jesus loved the church to the point of laying down His life for her, and that love goes on and on as he tirelessly nurtures her, encourages and considers her. He cherishes her and aims to make her the most beautiful expression of His love that she can be, reaching her full potential. Christian husbands, then and now, have a very hard act to follow!

Wives — choose to yield to your husband in love

'If you had a husband who behaved like Jesus, you wouldn't have any problems,' sighed Hilary. 'But when you're married to someone who doesn't even pretend to follow Him, that's an entirely different matter. And anyway what does submission *mean*? It sounds so archaic and wishy washy. I couldn't bring myself to be a doormat.'

The word does have a rather downtrodden ring to it doesn't it, but that's possibly because we give it meanings that it doesn't really have. So let's try to clarify what it doesn't mean before we grapple with what it does.

1. Submission doesn't demand that we put our husband in the place of authority or prominence that Jesus should have in our lives. Allegiance to Him comes first — always.

2. Submission doesn't mean that we should stop thinking for ourselves. God speaks to each one of us individually and it is up to us to respond for ourselves. This is equally important whether our husband *is* a Christian (because it stops us from getting lazy) or isn't (in which case he's liable to be deaf to God).

3. Submission doesn't mean that we can't influence our husband for good. Peter stresses the fact that an unbelieving partner can be drawn towards God by the positive spiritual qualities he sees in his wife. He does, however, warn against trying to nag or manipulate another person into God's Kingdom.

4. If a wife chooses to lovingly submit to her husband's leadership, there is no suggestion that she only does so because she is inadequate or inferior.

5. Submission isn't a role — who does the washing up or looks after the bank account or the children — but a relationship of mutual love and self-giving.

The challenge of being a 'Helpmeet'

Having seen what submission is not, let's see if we can sort out what it is, in the context of marriage. If a Christian husband is to reflect the attitude of Jesus, so too is the wife. Her role is just as demanding but different. She is asked to choose to give herself 100% to be a helpmeet. The word 'Helpmeet' is a strong word — in fact it's the same word as is used for the Holy Spirit. Sometimes He comforts and blesses, but at other times He confronts and challenges. She has the liberty to do all those things while cheerfully accepting her husband's leadership. The exception to that is when to follow his lead would cause her to disobey God. Like the Christian husband, she too has a model to follow in Jesus. Although He was equal with God He didn't hang on to that equality, but chose to lay it aside, and accept all the constraints of being human. Jesus said: 'I lay down my life...no one takes it from me, but I lay it down of my own accord.'

Jesus was equal with God, as a woman is equal with her husband, but He voluntarily responded to the Father's will. True submission *is* a voluntary thing. It is an attitude of the heart, not just of certain actions, and it can't be dragged from us by force. It has the potential to transform relationships, taking away all the elbowing for advantage and one-upmanship. Jesus said, 'If you cling to your life you will lose it, but if you give it up for me you will save it' (*Matthew 10:11*), and the same applies to our rights. Cling on to them and go the 'me first' route, and difficulties will follow as surely as night comes after day. God intends marriage to give completion to the two individuals involved, not competition.

Be a cheerful giver

We all know the difference between a gift given with joy and enthusiasm, and one that is offered purely from a sense of duty. And we all know which one we would rather have! Paul was writing to the Christians at Corinth about money when he said:

> **Remember this: whoever sows sparingly will also reap sparingly, and whoever sows generously will also reap generously. Each man should give what he has decided in his heart to give, not reluctantly or under compulsion for God loves a cheerful giver.**

But I think that we can read that as being true for the far more costly gift of ourselves. It may be very difficult to give joyfully rather than grudgingly, but we don't have to do it in our own strength, and we don't have fear running out of energy! Paul goes on to say:

> **And God is able to meet all grace abound to you, so that in all things at all times, having all that you need, you will abound in every good work.**

As marriage counsellor Dorothy Dennis points out, it's interesting to notice that God does things in the opposite way from the one we would naturally expect. He tells men to approach marriage from the heart and women from the head. Men are told to love and women are told to support and respect. The end result is that if this is done, both receive the things that they need, but which the other might not think of offering them!

'Is respect really so important to men?' queried

Louise. 'It sounds like pure Victoriana to me! Referring to your husband as 'Mr' and treating his word as law! Surely those days have long gone. In any case, respect is something that has to be earned, and if your husband doesn't uphold God's standards in his personal and business life, then it's very hard to respect him.'

It may be very difficult to
give joyfully rather than grudgingly,
but we don't have to do it in
our own strength, and we don't have
fear running out of energy!

Respecting his rights

Many people who aren't Christians live lives worthy of respect, and of course there are those, some of whom might claim to be Christians, who do not. But even when we can't respect our partner's actions, we can respect his God-given role and responsibilities as a husband, and as a man made in God's image with all the potential that that implies. We can encourage our children to respect his good points by focusing on these, and refraining from criticizing him to them. And we can respect the right he has to:

- hold and express his own opinions and feelings;
- be listened to with an open mind and taken seriously;
- set his own priorities;
- say yes or no for himself without being made to feel guilty or unacceptable;
- ask for what he wants;
- ask for information or advice;
- make mistakes and be wrong;

- have his physical and emotional needs met.

It is interesting that the sexual relationship is the only 'right' that the New Testament speaks about, in relation to marriage, and it is also an example of decision making between husband and wife.

> **The man should give his wife all that is her right as a married woman, and the wife should do the same to her husband: ...do not refuse these rights to each other. The only exception...would be the agreement of both husband and wife to refrain from the rights of marriage for a limited time, so that they can give themselves more completely to prayer.** *1 Corinthians 7:3 - 5*, Living Bible

Paul is obviously talking to couples where both are Christians here, but the general principle still holds good. When there is a high level of friction in a marriage, sexual relations often become a battleground, and understandably so. But even in this very sensitive area God can work a miracle. Here's just one example:

Meg was increasingly resentful of James' selfishness and lack of interest in her and their son. 'I wanted someone that I could share my life with,' she said, 'but how can you be a helpmeet to someone who is totally disinterested in sharing any sort of responsibility? Apart from the first twelve months of Rupert's life, I have always been the main breadwinner in our marriage. James had just got on with his own life as if we were nothing to do with him. Self-pity, anger and bitterness festered in me like a running sore, and our sex life dwindled to almost nothing.

'It was when my mother died, and I had prayer counselling to help me cope, that all these other emotions just erupted. I recognized the desert that we were in, and decided to give our relationship one last chance. I told God how sorry I was for all the anger and bitterness that I'd harboured, and asked Him to give me a new love for James.

'I wouldn't have believed that it was possible if I hadn't experienced it, but God gave us a kind of "second honeymoon". Over the couple of years since I prayed that prayer, James has gradually become more loving, sociable and communicative. Our physical relationship has become a joy and a real unifying factor. My one disappointment is that although James knows that I could only make the first move because God worked in me, he's still not prepared to turn to God himself.'

Respond realistically

It *is* very hard to carry out your side of the marriage commitment, when your partner is making little attempt to do the same. But God knows what is in our hearts and judges our attitudes. 'If the willingness is there, the gift is acceptable, according to what he has, not according to what he does not have,' said Paul. There again he was talking about money, but I think we can apply the principle more widely.

If we are trying to respect our partner's rights, it is natural enough to hope that he or she will do the same for us — and often this will be so. But if it is not? Sometimes it is right to simply die to our wants, and give way gracefully. Not all wrongs have to be corrected; not all privileges have to be insisted upon, not all hurts have to be aired. On these occasions we can simply trust God to work things out in His way, without our fighting for our agenda, and carry on 'washing the feet' of those we love, in a practical way.

But there are other times when enough is enough. If we are asked to love what God hates or hate what God loves, then we are right to refuse. Mary couldn't stop her husband accepting 'cash in hand' payments from clients, but she could and did refuse to lie to the accountant on his behalf. Lianne couldn't stop her husband bringing 'blue' videos into the house — although she did voice her unhappiness about it — but she could and did refuse to watch them with him. Lisa did all that she could to accommodate Tony's wishes. When he told her that he wanted them to spend summer Sundays sailing, she cheerfully got up in time for early Communion. When he wanted to entertain friends on 'House Group' night, she enrolled in a day-time Bible Study group. But when he said that he would leave her unless she gave up her faith altogether, she told him gently but firmly that that was something she would never do...and Tony stayed!

Reject discouragement

It is hard to maintain the hope that things will change, if we have been in a difficult situation for months or years, and nothing that we do or say seems to make any difference. But do you remember what happened when the disciples were faced with a crowd of 5,000 people and five small loaves and two small fish to feed them with? In their view it was a hopeless situation, but when Jesus took the food, blessed it, broke it into pieces and handed it out, it was more than adequate. Not only did everyone have enough, but there were supplies left over for others.

Sybil and Ted had been married fifteen years or more, and they had both been active Christians when they started life together. But gradually Ted's interest in spiritual things had been swamped by a demanding job, and he slowly moved from being totally committed to Jesus to being actively hostile, and mocking his wife's belief. Sybil clung on to her faith, but her love for Ted seemed to wither and die — in fact she admits that there were times when she actually wished him dead. Ted said that he wanted a divorce, and Sybil agreed. Just before they instructed a solicitor, Sybil listened to a tape that literally changed both their lives.

'The speaker talked about what Jesus could do with very little, if we would act in faith. I was riveted! I told God that I was sorry for my negative attitudes towards Ted. I asked Him to take the very little desire that I had for the marriage to continue, and the glimmer of affection that was left, and do something with it.

'God started answering my prayers. The Holy Spirit must have worked overtime in me and helped me to persevere, because I didn't *feel* any different for a long time. God helped me to act lovingly even though I felt nothing. Instead of eating with the children, and then "plonking" his dinner down in front of him, I made the effort to cook things that he liked, and sometimes sat down and ate with him. I tried to smile and take an intelligent interest in how his day had gone. Over the course of about a year, Ted began to do things to please me, and love grew again.'

Today Sybil and Ted are enjoying their retirement together, in a way that seemed impossible to imagine fifteen years ago. He is softer in his attitude towards Christian things, and Sybil is able to share encouragement and advice with other women who have uncommitted husbands, by running a support group in her church.

The version of Luke 6 verse 35 in the margin of my Bible has encouragement for all the 'Megs' and 'Sybils' among us — and for the rest of us too. 'Love your enemies and do them good, and lend, *despairing of no man*.' And veteran missionary Amy Carmichael's comment on that verse brooks no quibbling.

'If our Lord does not despair of us, we must not despair of ourselves. We must not say "I can't. Others can but...it is not in me to conquer. I shall be defeated to the end." That is folly and treachery too, for it is disbelieving the word of our God. His word is always "Fear not. You can. Have I not commanded thee? Be strong and of a good courage." Is there one discouraging word in our Bible? No! not one.'

12

Love That Cares

HOW TO LISTEN TO YOUR PARTNER

Every human being longs to be loved and understood and these basic needs walk hand in hand. If you understand someone it is much easier to love him; if you love him you really want to understand. And the vital link between the two is effective communication. The trouble is that communication is something that we often talk about, understand very little, and put into practice badly. In fact counsellors tell us that 80% of relationship problems stem from a basic lack of communication skills.

The very wise Christian writer, Paul Tournier, who was a general practitioner for many years, says,

> **It is impossible to over-emphasize the immense need men have to be really listened to, to be taken seriously, to be understood…No one can develop freely in this world and find a full life, without feeling understood by at least one person.**

Communication *is* a complicated subject. People write theses and books about it. But defined simply it is 'the imparting of news, information or feelings.' I have some news that I want you to be aware of, so I think about it, put my thoughts into words and speak. You hear and hopefully understand what I have said.

For that moment, I have become a transmitter, you have become a receiver, and the words that have passed between us have become the message. Communication has taken place!

It sounds so easy, doesn't it? But there are so many ways in which the whole process can go wrong. A Christian husband or wife may long to share the good news that they have discovered, but have difficulty in finding the right words. The bald facts may not be too difficult to express, but the feelings behind them are a much more sensitive matter. And so there is a fault in the transmitter. Or perhaps the not-yet-believing partner changes the subject every time anything remotely to do with God comes up. He or she obviously doesn't want to hear about such things and so the 'receiver' shuts down.

Many women complain that they find it very difficult to communicate with their partner in depth. On the whole, men prefer to talk about facts rather than feelings, and the heart to heart sharing that many women long for is more likely to happen with her women friends than her husband. It isn't possible to explore all the ways in which communication can be improved in one chapter, so we'll have to content ourselves with focusing on two of the main areas in which we can do better — really listening to what our partner has to say, and resolving conflict when it arises.

Become a better listener

Many psychiatrists would say that one of the greatest gifts we can give to anyone is to listen to them; not just to hear what they are saying, but to listen to them with love. And this applies to children just as much as it does to other adults. There are real skills involved in being a good listener — skills that anyone can learn, once we realize what they are.

• **Attitude is important.** The way we feel about the person to whom we are listening will colour what we hear. If we find him boring, irritating or tiresome, this attitude will distort what we hear, and may even filter out part of his message. In addition he will probably sense the lack of sympathy and find it hard to continue with what he wants to say. Acceptance of the other person is vital if we are really going to be able to listen properly.

• **Don't switch on to auto-pilot.** Did you know that we can listen five times faster than we can speak? This means that there are quite a few opportunities for our concentration to wander. During this time we may easily miss what is being said because we:

- are too busy thinking of what we want to say as soon as the other person draws breath
- ignore the things we don't want to hear and focus only on the points that seem important to us
- start thinking about our own problems!

• **Give your full attention.** Have you ever tried to talk to your husband in a restaurant while he constantly looks over your shoulder at the couple having a first class row two tables away? If so, you will know how difficult it is to maintain the flow of what you want to say. On the other hand, if he hangs on your every word, you immediately talk with ease.

Chrissie had a practical demonstration of this at a training session on listening skills that she went to recently. She was so struck by the freedom that she felt to speak, when listened to attentively, that she shared her discovery with Doris, who had often complained that her husband had little to say. Doris was very dubious, but decided to try it out on her husband as soon as she had the opportunity, if only to prove to Chrissie that it wouldn't work in her situation.

A few days later, Doris was reading when her husband came into the room and made a casual comment about what he had been doing in the garden. Doris seized her chance. Instead of glancing up from her book, she put it down, swung her legs up onto the settee, and gave her husband her full attention. To her amazement, he talked non-stop for the next hour.

• **Listen with your eyes and heart as well as with your ears.** When we are listening to someone it isn't just our ears that need to be 'switched on'. When we are speaking we only express 7% of our meaning through the words we use. That's difficult to believe but true, according to people who analyze these things! Then we communicate 38% of our meaning through our tone of voice, and 55% in the way we stand, sit, smile, scowl, twiddle hair, clench our fists and otherwise tie ourselves into knots. So it is crucial that we watch the body language that our partner uses. Touch is important too. Your partner may assure you that he is perfectly happy for you to go on the church weekend, but if you put your arm around him and he is stiff and unyielding, take notice!

• **Be prepared to listen in silence.** Most of the time we don't want to hear another person's remedy for our dilemma! One of the most helpful things that we can do for someone who has a problem is to listen quietly while they struggle to put their feelings into words, giving the occasional nod, or word of encouragement to show that we are still listening. So try not to:

- Come up with instant solutions — 'If I were you I'd... He is asking to be heard and understood. If he wants practical help he will let you know.
- Use 'door shutters' — ending the conversation with 'Don't worry', 'You'll soon feel better.' He may not want to be soothed so much as to know that you feel the hurt with him. To identify with our partner in that way is to be Christ-like. He shares our pain.
- Diagnose the cause of his problem with, 'What you really mean is', 'You feel like that because...' Your job at that point is to understand *what* he feels. *Why* he feels it is up to him to discover. You may be asked for your opinion or help about that. You may not. That is up to your partner.

• **When necessary be a reflective listener.** Listening quietly and with our full attention, is always a very important part of helping someone to unload emotional pressures or to sort out a problem. But sometimes it is not enough on its own. This is where reflective listening skills come in. Sometimes we need to repeat what we've heard in our own words, to make sure that what we think we have heard is actually what the speaker said. We do this automatically when we are given instructions about how to find our way somewhere. At other times it may be helpful to reflect the emotions that seem to underlie what is being said.

Imagine that your partner is complaining about the fact that you want to give some money to the church building fund. You might want to reflect back with: 'Let me just be clear about what you're saying. You don't want any money from our joint account to be given?' (clarifying the facts), 'But would you be unhappy if I gave some of my spending money for the project?'

In reflective listening you are doing several things:

- you aren't telling him how he should or shouldn't feel.
- you show him that you want to understand how he feels, even though you may not agree with those feelings.
- you don't defend yourself or attack him.
- you ask for clarification in order to understand better (not to fight your own corner) with words like 'are you saying that?' 'Can you give me an example of what you mean?'

• **Recognize that there is a right time and place for this kind of intensive listening.** Listening is hard work and most of us find there are times when this degree of concentration and self-giving is almost impossible. If we're very tired, frustrated or pre-occupied with our own problems, all our available energy is used up in listening to ourselves!

You know what it's like when you've both had a bad day. When you catch up with one another in the evening, you're in no mood to listen to his woes, until you've unloaded your aggravation about the children, the mechanic at the garage or your impossible boss. And he feels the same way. Which is where the saying, 'Never discuss a problem standing up or on an empty stomach' must have come from! Choose the right time and place for heart to heart sharing and it can be of great benefit to you both. Pick the wrong moment, and you could end up with a first class fight. Which brings us to the kind of communication that most of us avoid like the plague — conflict!

Don't let your anger lead you into sin

Every close relationship has its share of difficulties and disagreements — and Christians aren't exempt. We are just as likely to have to deal with conflict as anyone else — particularly if we have an uncommitted partner. The Bible recognizes that we all struggle in this area, and has plenty to say about how we should act and react to one another.

One of the key passages is in Paul's letter to the Ephesians, in which he says:

> No more lying, then! Everyone must tell the truth...if you become angry, do not let your anger lead you into sin, and do not stay angry all day. Don't give the devil a chance...Do not use harmful words, but only helpful words, the kind that build up and provide what is needed, so that what you say will do good to those who hear you. And do not make God's Holy Spirit sad...Get rid of all bitterness, passion and anger. No more shouting or insults, no more hateful feelings of any sort. Instead be kind and tender-hearted to one another and forgive one another as God has forgiven you through Christ.   *Ephesians 4:25-32*, GNB

Did you notice that Paul assumes that there will be times when we will be angry, and that that in itself is not wrong? Anger is natural; it's what we do with our anger that is the vital issue. Very often Christians feel guilty about being angry and try to suppress it. When we do this it's like pushing the anger down into a rubbish sack, and using the guilty feelings as a tie to prevent the anger from bubbling out. The trouble is that by doing this we are merely burying these emotions alive.

As the days pass, irritations large and small are

added, and the 'sack' becomes so heavy that we're weighed down by our grievances. Eventually they will build up so much pressure that the 'sack' will burst, and the anger will erupt with enormous force, because it has been compressed and suppressed for so long.

Let's take a peep at Lorna and Terry's house early in the morning. Lorna has slipped out of bed early, and goes downstairs to spend time with God. She becomes so absorbed in what she's reading, that she fails to notice that the alarm, which she usually re-sets, hasn't gone off in the bedroom above. Eventually she realizes that the house is uncannily quiet, dashes round to wake the children and Terry and they all start the day in a rush.

In her haste, Lorna burns the toast, and finds that they are now out of bread, because Terry had forgotten to buy some the previous day (his job). Terry leaves his dirty clothes all over the bedroom floor and runs down to breakfast wearing his least favourite shirt, because Lorna went to pray with a friend the evening before, instead of doing the ironing (her job). At this point, neither say anything, but they both have a number of items in their respective 'sacks' — and it's only 8.15 a.m.! After breakfast, Terry grinds his teeth because Lorna has squeezed the toothpaste tube in the middle — again; Lorna simmers because the shower is clogged up with hairs and the shampoo bottle is minus its cap and gets knocked over. The grievance sacks become heavier!

And so it goes on for several days with pressures at work, problems with the children and a sharp short phone call from Granny because they've forgotten to enquire about the outcome of her visit to the doctor, all adding weight to those invisible bags. Eventually one more annoyance gets pushed into the 'sack' and it gives

*Lorna simmers because the shower is clogged up with hairs . . .
the grievance sack becomes heavier.*

at the seams, so that all the anger comes tumbling out
in a furious row.

That isn't the biblical solution! We need to deal with
our grievances immediately if we can, and if that isn't
possible, as soon after the event as is reasonably possible. Otherwise we end up with a relationship that
resembles my fridge when it needs defrosting — full of
little containers of leftovers which, having been pushed
to the back of the shelves, are now distinctly nasty! If
you're not sure how to bring the subject up again, try,
'I've been thinking about what happened the other day
when...' or, 'You know what you said about...' or simply, 'I've got a problem.'

Attack the problem, not your partner

'Do not use harmful words, but only helpful words...' says Paul. The trouble is that harmful words come to our minds so much more readily than helpful ones when we're angry, don't they? But harmful words degrade and destroy the dignity of the person you are talking to; they tear down his self-esteem. There may be times when criticism is necessary, but it also needs to be constructive, truthful and spoken in love. Some of us have a tendency to blurt things out without thinking. A lot of damage would be prevented if we would habitually ask ourselves, 'This may need to be said, but does it need saying now? Is it true, is it kind, is it necessary?'

Helpful words don't exaggerate — 'You always...', 'You never...'. Nor do they hit below the belt — bringing up old injuries from the past, or homing in on weak spots that you know he is struggling to deal with. When we are seeking the good of another person we will refrain from brow-beating one another with words or uncontrolled temper. We will not manipulate by using tears as a weapon, or punish by withdrawing into long periods of silence, withholding sex or doing other things that will make life unpleasant.

Be kind ... and tender-hearted ... and forgiving

The words kind, tender-hearted, forgiving, don't reflect the attitude of most of us when we're in a conflict situation, do they? We tend to rush in, stoutly defending our point of view at any cost, and the result is often damaged relationships and entrenched positions. So even if we feel that right is on our side, it's worth trying to tackle the problem in God's way.

God's way is to listen and love and forgive, over and over again, and only He can help us to handle our anger like that. He never holds grudges or throws past mistakes back in our face. When He forgives, He forgets and we, too, should be forgiving people, remembering at all times how much we have been forgiven. Some of us find it very hard to let a bone of contention go. But Jesus said that we should put things right between ourselves, and then consider the matter closed. (*Matthew 5:23*)

It's true that our partner may not be able to handle things in this way, without the grace of God to draw on. Chrissie found that Colin tended to sulk when he was angry, and would sometimes refuse to speak to her for days at a time. It was hard not to let his attitude shape hers. But grudges are like acid that will corrode and eventually destroy a relationship, and may give us stomach ulcers into the bargain! We save ourselves a lot of pain if we let them drop.

A Christian writer of long ago, said this about the formation of a natural pearl:

> 'A piece of grit or a grain of sand comes into the world of the oyster; something that intrudes and hinders and injures...but the pearl is the answer, by the injured of the injury done.'

Since I read that, I've been asking myself, 'Are the conflicts and problems in my life producing pearls or ulcers?' It's very much in my hands, for it all depends on the reaction of the injured to the injury done.

13

What About The Children?

SHARING OUR FAITH WITH OUR CHILDREN

Just as no one gets married intending to be unhappy, so no one embarks on parenthood planning to be a bad parent. Quite the reverse. Most of us imagine that we'll be perfect parents of model children — and get rather a nasty shock when the baby arrives and we discover what a huge task we've undertaken! Of course, we do our best to see that our children are properly fed, clothed, have friends to play with and toys and activities to stimulate their minds. But until we discover or rediscover a personal faith, any input we make to encourage spiritual development is likely to be a rather hit and miss affair. Once we experience God's love and reality for ourselves however, it becomes very important to us to share this dimension of life with our children as well as with our partner. What we may be less clear about, is how that can be done.

I won't have them brain-washed!

The reaction of an unbelieving partner to teaching children about God varies enormously. Colin couldn't understand Chrissie's desire to send their children to Sunday School, and later to go along with them herself, but he assumed that it would be a passing phase — for the children, at least — and so was prepared to accept the arrangement.

Paul was an open-minded man who felt that a knowledge of Christianity was part of his children's birthright. Since he didn't know enough to teach them himself, he was happy for Jenny to take them to church. He even went along himself from time to time to 'set a good example' as he saw it. The only condition that he asked Jenny to agree to, was that their attendance should be voluntary, once they reached secondary school age.

Steve saw the issue rather differently. He tended to use the children's church attendance as a weapon with which to punish Sue, and so, while he didn't object to them going openly, he regularly arranged to do things which the children would enjoy, and then encouraged them to 'have fun with Dad'.

Terry was more honest. He was a convinced atheist, and when Lorna first committed her life to Jesus, resolutely opposed the idea of her taking their children to church — unless they asked to go — or teaching them about her faith at home. However they did agree that when the children asked questions they would both answer honestly, from their own viewpoint.

Where do we go from here?

The Bible tells us that even those people who have never been taught about God sense something about His existence through His creation. And what folk like Terry fail to realize is that children develop spiritually just as they do physically, emotionally and mentally, whether we take active steps to shape that development or not. In refusing to allow formal input into that development, Terry was acting like the wicked witch in the fairy story who refused to have any flowers planted in her garden, and then found that the wind had blown the seeds over the wall anyway!

Look at the positives

You have almost certainly got some common ground that you can work on, in agreeing the standards you want to establish in your life together as a family. A recent survey shows that the majority of parents think honesty and reliability are very important, and see them as key values that they would like their children to hold.

Most of us would also want our children to respect us, and to hold human life as sacred. We would want them to understand that although people may sometimes fail to live up to the ideal, commitment to one's marriage partner, valuing another's good name and refraining from stealing their property are the foundation blocks of a healthy society. So although both parents may not share an active faith, recognizing that we agree with most of the Ten Commandments, must be a good place to begin, as we think about a framework for the children's moral and spiritual upbringing.

Recognize that a child's faith develops in stages

A baby is born with the potential to grow to a certain height, understand complicated ideas and form loving relationships with other people. He is also born with the capacity to believe in, trust, and actively follow God. But he has to grow and develop in all these areas — a newborn infant and a teenager are very different creatures.

In the first seven years or so of life, we are laying the foundations on which a more adult faith can be built. Faith is a difficult word to explain, but it may help if we think of it as a three-legged stool. The three crucial elements of faith — belief, trust in the object of that belief, and actions which stem from what we believe — are like the legs. They are all vital if the stool is going to be usable, but a baby or small child develops the 'trust' leg first.

When they are cared for by loving and dependable adults, children will gradually be able to understand that God is loving and dependable. As they learn from experience that parents, whom they can see, can be trusted, they are more likely to be able to trust the Heavenly Father that they can't see. God is the perfect parent, and in His dealings with us He demonstrates:

- Unconditional love and acceptance
- Absolute and ungrudging forgiveness
- Untiring commitment
- Protection and provision for our needs
- Consistent standards for behaviour
- Absolute freedom within clearly defined limits.

This gives us a pattern to follow. And the exciting thing is that if, with His help, we try to show those attitudes to our children, we are teaching them invaluable lessons about God without them setting foot in a church. These early years belong to what has been called the stage of *experienced faith*. Little children form their patterns of believing, trusting and doing, from what they experience and learn from others. Lorna found this a great comfort when Terry was so opposed to her teaching the children about spiritual things in a direct way.

The diagram overleaf, taken from *Children Finding Faith*, published by Scripture Union, shows how these foundations of shared trust, love and care can lead to faith:

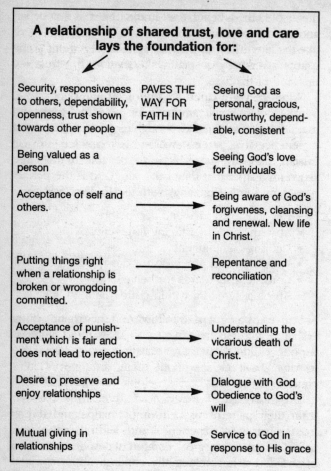

A relationship of shared trust, love and care lays the foundation for:

	PAVES THE WAY FOR FAITH IN	
Security, responsiveness to others, dependability, openness, trust shown towards other people	→	Seeing God as personal, gracious, trustworthy, dependable, consistent
Being valued as a person	→	Seeing God's love for individuals
Acceptance of self and others.	→	Being aware of God's forgiveness, cleansing and renewal. New life in Christ.
Putting things right when a relationship is broken or wrongdoing committed.	→	Repentance and reconciliation
Acceptance of punishment which is fair and does not lead to rejection.	→	Understanding the vicarious death of Christ.
Desire to preserve and enjoy relationships	→	Dialogue with God Obedience to God's will
Mutual giving in relationships	→	Service to God in response to His grace

From *Children Finding Faith* by Francis Bridger, © Scripture Union, used by permission.

Move forward at the child's own pace

Lorna had a particularly difficult situation to deal with, but most not-yet-believing parents are happy for their partner to share what they believe with the children, so long as it isn't forced down their throats. Little children punctuate the day with questions. So, especially if we are at home with under-fives, there will be plenty of opportunity to talk to them quite naturally about Jesus, simply by taking the openings as they arise. You know the kind of thing.

'Why are you reading that book, Mummy?'

'This is God's special book; it's called the Bible and it tells us all about Him.'

'Who is God?' is a natural lead in to explaining God in terms of creation; something even a small child can begin to grasp.

Of course, questions won't be reserved for times when you're doing 'religious' activities. Small children ask the most unexpected things at times and take our replies very literally. Pat was sorting out baby clothes with her three-year-old's help. William wanted to know what would happen to all his little brother's things, and Pat explained that they would give some away and keep some in case they had another baby.

'Are we going to have another baby then?' asked William. This was a bit of a poser, as Pat and her husband were still debating that point.

'We'll have to ask God about that,' his mother replied.

'I want to ask Him now,' said William. Somewhat taken aback, Pat prayed a brief prayer, asking God to let them know if He was going to send them another baby one day. Her telephone age child opened his eyes and looked at her expectantly.

'Did He say yes or no?' he demanded.

As children grow to junior and pre-teen age, their developing ability to think and reason come into play, and direct teaching about faith, brings the 'belief' leg of the stool into prominence. Some have a greater need to reason things out for themselves than others, and think very deeply from an early age. These children in particular need to feel that asking searching questions won't make them less lovable or acceptable than their more easy-going brothers and sisters.

I'd been reading our two older sons a bed-time story and was about to pray with them when Angus, who was then aged four, fixed me with a considering stare and said, 'You tell me all this about God, but how do I know that you're telling me about the right god. One of the false gods might be the real one.' Before I could gather my wits to reply, six-year-old David said reassuringly, 'But it must be true Angus, because if not, who made the world?' I decided that that was as good an answer as he was likely to get at that moment!

So questions come and go, and get even more complicated as the children grow older. We may even find questions that we are still wrestling with ourselves being raised. When this happens we can safely admit that this still puzzles us, and say something like, 'Yes, I've wondered about that too and think that it might be…' It is a good principle to keep answers short and to the point, recognizing that we are quite likely to have to answer the same question many times before the answer is finally grasped. But in an effort to be simple, we need to avoid saying anything we may have to unsay later.

There are, of course, many questions about life and belief that don't have a simple complete answer, and there will be times when we will have to admit that we don't know. If the answer can be found, then we can look for it together; if it is one of life's imponderables then we need to say so, assuring them at the same time that God is all knowing and can safely be left to care for those things. This may sound trite but it is true and a step of trust that we all have to take.

Share the burden with the church family

At this stage it is ideal if our children can be part of a lively worshipping church community, because they need to experience the reality and relevance of God in people's day to day lives, as well as learning the facts about Him. If we are already active Christians when the children are small, church-going will probably be a natural thing which has always been part of life as they know it.

It is a good principle to keep answers short and to the point, recognizing that we are quite likely to have to answer the same question many times before the answer is finally grasped

---

If, however, we come to faith when they are older, they may or may not be willing to join us in our worship. But in either case it's wise to consider the children's needs as well as our own when we think of which church we will go to. Sometimes there isn't a choice. We may have to go to the nearest church that is within walking distance or on a bus route. But if we can choose we will want to ask:

- Does this church have a family service or well-taught children's classes?
- Does it have mid-week activities, or organizations that my children would enjoy...a youth club, football team, etc.
- Do I know other families who go there with children of similar ages?

This last point is especially important, because families who go to church are very much in the minority these days and children hate to be different. It makes it a lot easier if children have school friends who are also church friends, and vice versa. Being the same as everyone else is a comfort zone we all lean towards, especially in the pre-teen and teenage years. The stage of faith development where they accept and believe what family or friends believe, without necessarily thinking it out in detail for themselves, has been described as *affiliative* faith. Some people never progress from there, even as adults!

As our children move through their teens, they are likely to reach the point where they start to question what they have been taught so far, and actively search for answers. It is at that point that *searching faith* hopefully becomes *owned* faith, where the teenagers or young adults accept Jesus for themselves. They will then begin to live out the implications of their faith from choice, because that is what they really believe. This is where the 'doing' leg of the three-legged faith stool comes into its own.

What about school?

What happens if school teaches one thing and you another? In a sense, this clash of views has to come sometime, and every child has to face it. It can start early these days with the celebration of festivals like Hallowe'en and multi-faith assemblies in junior school. Many parents are uneasy about their children participating, but afraid of making them unpopular with the staff if they create a fuss. This is where united and prayerful action can be helpful.

Lorna and Sally's children went to the same school, and they decided that they would go and see the head-mistress together about the school's plan for Hallowe'en right at the beginning of the autumn term.

They explained why they were unhappy about the pagan festival, and asked if their children could be given some work to do which related to All Saints' Day. Imagine their joy when a number of the teachers decided to make this their theme, instead of witches and ghosts! They also met to pray for the school once each term, and gradually a number of other Christian parents joined them, and their influence became a real force for good in the school.

As children grow older they do become increasingly aware that the Christian faith isn't the only belief system on offer. They can't avoid doing so because the National Curriculum now includes the study of other faiths. Some Christian parents worry in case this has a corrupting influence on their children. My feeling is that knowledge in itself isn't harmful, but simply gives a basis for clear-sighted choice. Of course it's helpful if we are well-informed ourselves, so that we can discuss the pros and cons with our children. But as teenagers often find it easier to talk to someone less emotionally involved than Mum or Dad, we can also actively encourage them to talk to another Christian adult, rather than feeling slighted or shut out if they do so.

The troubled years

Many of us wonder how we will cope when our children reach the dreaded teens. We read about drugs, drinking, under-age sex and unemployment and the future can look very frightening, especially if we have different views from our partner about how such things should be handled. It's impossible to give detailed guidance about this stage of family life because youngsters are all different. Some bob along from thirteen to nineteen and make hardly a ripple, whilst others cause headaches and heartaches for years. But there are some general principles which can help us.

• **Agreed policy.** We need to do our best to agree on acceptable behaviour with our partner, even if it isn't exactly as we might like it. Having done so, we need to stick to it and back one another up at all times. All children need the security of united parents, especially in their teens. Although they may kick against the rules laid down for them, it is nevertheless a welcome safety barrier behind which to retreat, when peer pressure gets too hot to handle.

• **Listen.** All children need to be listened to, but if there is one period when we need to sharpen up our listening skills, it's when we have teenagers. He or she needs to be listened to in the same way, and every bit as regularly as our partner does. Communication is an invaluable bridge over troubled water, but it takes time, availability (ours and theirs), patience, a respect for their rights to hold opinions with which we might disagree, and unshockability!

• **Respect.** As we respect our teenagers' right to hold their own opinions, we can reasonably expect them to do the same for us. At the point where we may hold different views on matters of faith and conduct from our partner, we need to learn to express that to the rest of the family, without criticizing them or being defensive ourselves.

• **Take care.** If our teenagers have accepted Jesus for themselves, we need to be aware of the danger of appearing to gang up with them, against our partner. It is very easy to share confidences, activities and interests in this situation, and in doing so make the other parent feel excluded and isolated.

• **Pray!** We can do our best, in our own strength, to guide our family life according to God's principles and perhaps produce reasonably happy and well balanced offspring. But if we are to help our children to find their place in God's Kingdom, embracing His plan for their life and serving Him with joy and conviction, the whole operation has to be bathed in prayer.

We need to pray that God will work in our lives so that we can be, in His strength, the sort of parent He can use. And then that He will enable us to bring every day, and every challenge in that day, to Him for His guidance and help. The whole of life as a parent is a process of loving and letting go. We have succeeded when we have done ourselves out of a job. So the final prayer target is that we will do all that we can to introduce our children to a loving Heavenly Father, and then have the courage to stand back and release them into His all-knowing and all-loving care, saying with Paul:

> I am...full of confidence because I know whom I have trusted, and I am sure that He is able to keep safe until that Day what I have entrusted to him.
>
> *2 Timothy 1:12*, GNB

14

Soul Survivor

THE SECRET OF ACCEPTANCE

I t is a desperately difficult thing to live in an atmosphere of constant criticism and disapproval. Christians with partners who don't share their beliefs often feel very sad because they can't share this most precious and foundational part of their life with the one they love. It does inevitably have an effect on their relationship. But they don't necessarily have any more (or any fewer) problems in their marriage than someone for whom faith differences aren't an issue. However there *are* those who experience real hostility and opposition because of their faith. They have a hard and lonely road to tread.

Jesus was realistic about the tensions and difficulties that could arise for a Christian, even within their own family circle. 'Happy are those,' he said, 'who are persecuted because they do what God requires;...Happy are you when people insult you and persecute you and tell all kinds of evil lies against you because you are my followers. Be happy and glad, for a great reward is kept for you in heaven.' (*Matthew 5:10,11*, GNB)

Jackie felt her 'lone Christian' status within her marriage very deeply, because she and her husband Alan had both started married life as enthusiastic followers of Jesus. But since Alan's faith had grown cold she often felt as if she was facing real persecution, and it was very difficult to feel happy about it.

'I'm cold shouldered continually for going out — again — and for being late in...although I'm always back by 10.30, and Alan isn't an early to bed person. Last night I went to say goodbye before I left for house group and he just turned away saying, "I suppose you'll bother to come home some time!" And yet when Alan has an evening playing snooker, he comes home any time up to 1 a.m., regardless of the fact that I have to be up early for work. He constantly criticizes my church friends, and that hurts. But the worst thing is when he mocks all the things about God that were once so precious to him — I sometimes wonder how God refrains from judging him in some terrible way there and then.'

There are no pat formulae, which, if followed will automatically transform a hostile partner into a loving and supportive one. Only the grace of God can do that. But there are certain practical steps which people in this situation have found helpful.

Accentuate the positive

'My friends at church go on about how difficult life at home must be for me,' said Clare, 'but sometimes I feel sorry for them. They don't seem to make any decisions on their own, and I sometimes wonder whether their faith rests on their partner or on Jesus. When I'm under pressure, or I have a decision about my spiritual life to make, I can't lean on Robin, so I have to turn to God. I feel a bit like a plant in a drought. I have to drive my roots down deep to survive, so in some ways I feel that I'm better off. And there's nothing like having a partner who watches you constantly to see if you live up to what you believe, to keep you on your toes spiritually!

Of course I want Robin to discover a vital and living faith for himself. But in the mean time I'm learning things I wouldn't have had to think about if my situation was different.'

Be complete as one

'Life at our church is so couple oriented,' complained Sue. 'If you come alone, you can so easily feel only half a Christian. I just long for the day when Steve comes to believe so that I can be active and involved and really grow as a Christian.'

If we are the sole representative of Jesus within our family, then there will inevitably be some restrictions on what we can do within the church. However, we need to guard against putting our own spiritual life and growth on hold until such a time as we can go forward with our partner. In one sense we are all 'lone Christians'. No one else can have a relationship with Jesus for us. And just as we often wish away the years when our children are small — when he sleeps through the night…starts to walk…begins school…I'll be able to enjoy parenthood, we say, so we can waste our lives waiting for our partner to come to faith.

There can come a turning point. The American author, Linda Davis, described how she came to the decision to live each day positively in her book, *How to be the Happy Wife of an Unsaved Husband*:

> I read Hanna Hurnard's book *Hind's Feet on High Places*. The unhappy little 'Much Afraid' was led into a…desert by the Chief Shepherd. She never saw a living thing there until one day…she discovered a small golden flower blooming happily, all alone. When asked its name the flower

replied 'Behold me! My name is "Acceptance-with-joy"!'

I, too, eventually learned the secret of acceptance with joy in the midst of my desert experience. I was sick of being miserable. Something inside me said, 'I'm tired of waiting to be happy. If my husband doesn't get saved until he's ninety-nine years old, look at all the years I will have wasted being miserable about it. This is my life and I'm not going to waste any more of it being unhappy about something I have no power to change. I'm just going to have to accept what I can't change and be happy in spite of it!'

It finally dawned on me that life is not made up of 'somedays' but of thousands of 'todays'. If I wanted to enjoy my life I had to enjoy it and be happy *today*, regardless of circumstances and no matter what my husband's spiritual condition. I had to accept, totally, the fact that my husband was not a believer and live with it happily. No more being forlorn in church...and no more thinking of myself as an inferior Christian. I began to hold my head up high and prove to the world that a woman is no less of a person because she is alone — not even in church. She is not half of a pair; she is complete in Christ.

Jackie came to that conclusion eventually too. 'I realized that the tighter I hung on to Alan and tried to draw him back into church with me, the more he would resist,' she said. 'He was God's problem, not mine. So I made up my mind to release him to go his own way. I choose not to feel guilty about going to church and to home group, although I don't overdo it. And I try not to imply by word or action that he should think of joining me. I'm learning to let his negative comments slide over me rather than taking them to heart. If he criticizes the church or my friends, I simply say something like, "I can't agree with you there," and let the matter drop. And once he realized that he couldn't wind me up like he had been doing, some of the heat went out of the situation.'

If we are the sole representative
of Jesus within our family,
then there will inevitably be
some restrictions on what we
can do within the church

Spot the Enemy

'When I reached out to God,' said Gillian, 'it wasn't one of those cloud nine experiences that you sometimes hear about. George was working very long hours, and drinking heavily as a way of dealing with the pressure. I had three small children and lived miles away from my family in a village where I had very few friends. George was working most Sunday mornings and so I started going to church occasionally and was then invited to a day time Bible study group during the week. I didn't understand half of what was being said, but I felt that if God could make my life even a bit better, it was worth a try. So I prayed a prayer that basically said, "If you can do anything with a messed up person like me, here I am," and didn't tell anyone for a while.

'I can't say that my life at home got any better — in fact, it got worse once George realized that I wanted to go to church regularly. I discovered from his mother that he had been very badly treated by some Christians when he was at school, and the mere mention of anything to do with God drove him wild. I had my Bible thrown across the room, Christian books torn up, and I'm not exaggerating when I say that it seemed as if Satan himself was looking out of his eyes when George ranted and raved at me. The language he used, and the things he said were not what the man I fell in love with and married would ever have said.'

Satan...provoking someone to uncharacteristic behaviour...does that all sound rather extreme and alarming? Gillian's experience is by no means unique. Several other women and at least one man have told me about violent reactions to the mention of spiritual things, or perhaps a sense of spiritual oppression in the home when their partner is around. It shouldn't really surprise us because the Bible is very clear about the existence of evil, and the fact that this world of ours is the realm in which Satan operates. Human beings are either part of the Kingdom of Jesus, or under the dominion of Satan. The apostle John spells this out very clearly in his first epistle when he writes:

> **We know that we are children of God, and that the whole world is under the control of the evil one.** *1 John 5:19*

Satan certainly doesn't want to lose any of those who are under his power, and so he blinds them to spiritual realities, and holds them in spiritual bondage. This may sound like a situation that we can do little about, until we grasp the fact that as Christians we have authority over Satan, because Jesus defeated him when He died on the cross. We don't have to cringe or cower because 'the Spirit who is in you is more powerful than the spirit in those who belong to the world.'

The armour of God

We can go on the offensive against Satan, but before we do, we need to put on the spiritual armour which will protect and equip us for a spiritual battle. In Ephesians chapter six, Paul is very specific about what we are up against when he says: 'We are not fighting against human beings but against the wicked spiritual forces in the heavenly world, the rulers, authorities and cosmic powers of this dark age.'

We will need to wear:

• **Truth as a belt.** Satan constantly tries to distort God's truth, and so we need to understand what we believe, in order to counter his lies.

• **Righteousness as our breastplate.** When we're sure that we're righteous in God's eyes because of what Jesus has done, we're protected from guilt and the condemnation that Satan loves to heap on us.

• **Shoes.** We need to be always ready to announce the Good News of Jesus, wherever we go.

• **Faith as a shield.** In New Testament times, the shield was wooden, large enough to protect the whole body, and often soaked in water so that flaming arrows would be doused on contact.

• **Salvation as a helmet.** This will protect the mind against doubt. The first temptation was 'Did God really tell you...?'

• **The word of God.** The sword of the Spirit.

The sword is the only offensive weapon that is mentioned in this list, but it is all we need. When we pray against Satan, using the authority invested in us by Jesus and the promises He has given to us in His word, we are using His weapons and they have 'the divine power to demolish strongholds' (2 Corinthians 10:4).

The exact words you use don't really matter, as long as you realize that you are praying with the authority of Jesus, as you speak in His name. But if you find it helpful to have a pattern of words, you might like to adapt the following to your own situation:

> You demons who are seeking to lead astray, hold in bondage and finally destroy my beloved...I bind you in the name of Jesus Christ. I am seated with Him in spiritual authority, and say to you 'Take your hands off...life. Release his will so that he will be free to accept and then serve Jesus as his Lord and Saviour.'
>
> By the power of the shed blood of Jesus Christ, I come against the strongholds...[of rebellion, unbelief, bitterness...] that Satan has erected in the mind of...I cast down these strongholds and every high thing which exalts itself against the knowledge of God. I release that mind to obedience to Christ. I loose it to be reconciled to God. In the mighty name of Jesus.

Into the wilderness

One of the most painful experiences that a married Christian can have is when his or her partner turns away from the faith they once shared together. The degree of backsliding seems to vary. Some people walk right away from the church and deny any faith at all. They often then become very hostile to their partner's belief. Others 'follow from afar' — still coming to church from time to time or even regularly to 'keep up appearances' — but in their heart are very lukewarm, and critical of any determination their partner might have to go on with God.

Caroline felt that she had experienced the worst of

both worlds. 'Philip came to faith six years after I did,' she said, 'and I was over the moon. It had been such a difficult period, and there were times when I wondered whether our marriage would stand the strain. Then he had a serious accident and while he was in hospital, wondering if he would ever walk again, he told God that He could have what was left of his life, such as it was. He did walk again and grew in his faith very rapidly. He is a very clear-thinking and competent man, and I think that this is where the trouble started. Our church was short of men who could take responsibility, and before Philip had been a Christian for a year, he was one of the leadership team. He was encouraged to run before he could walk, and the inevitable happened — he fell flat on his face!

'He was quick to see that what we professed and what we did didn't always match up. For instance, at the first church business meeting he ever attended he asked why, if the church's mission was evangelism, we were only giving 10% of our budget to it. It was a genuine question, but it didn't please our minister. And so gradually Philip became disillusioned, and because he was too proud to admit that he needed help, he slipped quietly into a backwater. We moved to a new area, and he came to our neighbourhood church reasonably regularly, but with only minimal commitment, and he didn't like me to get too involved.'

Caroline began to find that her own relationship with God was being affected. When Philip increasingly found reasons why they should do things that clashed with going to church on Sunday, she felt that she was faced with a choice. 'It was as if I was at a crossroads,' she said. 'If I went Philip's way, I would mark time spiritually — or in reality slip back, because you can't stand still in the Christian life. But if I went down the other path I ran the risk of leaving him behind. As I prayed about it, I felt as if God was saying, "You aren't accountable for Philip's decisions but you are responsible for your own — you follow Me."

'I wondered at first if I'd got it right, until I realized that Philip knew the truth and was still God's child, although a rebellious one. I'd always tried to explain away his lack of involvement, but it seemed as if God said, "Stop covering up for him. Take the hedge away so that I can deal with the situation in My way." From that point on I stopped making excuses for Philip. If he didn't come to church and someone asked where he was, I simply said, "He didn't feel like coming today", and left it at that.'

Caroline, too, had to come to a point of acceptance. 'I realized that deep down I was very angry with Philip because I felt that he had let me down,' she said. 'One night I couldn't sleep and as I sat downstairs in the dark, I sensed that I needed to forgive Philip for not keeping all the promises he'd made when he first became a Christian, and to repent of my anger and bitterness. And as I prayed for strength to do that, I faced the fact that things might not change. "Lord," I wept, "if this is as good as our life together is going to get, give me the courage to accept it and the wisdom to know how to live with it, without fretting for change all the time. Show me how to be victorious — one day at a time.'

The grass is always greener!

Gina spent ten long years following Jesus alone, whilst her husband Roger busied himself with his career and his hobbies. 'I don't know if it would have been any easier if we'd never shared our faith,' she said. 'But we had had such a deep and supportive relationship to start with. We'd prayed together; worked in the church together and even thought about going overseas as missionaries — and then we lost it all. I felt as if I'd been spiritually widowed, and like other widows I knew what I was missing. The temptation to look for another man to replace Roger's spiritual input was sometimes overwhelming.'

Christians aren't immune to sexual temptation. And if our partner is disinterested or even hostile towards the things we long to share, it is very easy to become emotionally involved with someone who will understand. Gina learned this lesson the hard way.

'Things had been very difficult at home,' she said. 'Roger was so moody and preoccupied, and the child that I longed for just didn't materialize. To try and take my mind off things I got involved with the missions support group at church. We had a year of fund-raising events to help some of our church youngsters go overseas on a work party in the summer holidays. Jeff, the youth leader, and I dreamed up all sorts of mad schemes, and it was all such fun.

'Our planning meetings got longer and more frequent, and then it seemed necessary to meet for lunch. We started to talk about what we could do for God if I wasn't married, and although outwardly I was saying "We shouldn't talk like this," inwardly I was saying, "Yes! take me away from my situation." It wasn't until my friend Kate commented on how much time Jeff and I were spending together that I realized how close to the rocks we were drifting.

'It was agonizingly embarrassing, but somehow I managed to be honest with Kate about my thoughts and yearnings. I couldn't pull out of the group immediately without causing a lot of comment, but as there were only eight more weeks before the youngsters went away, I committed myself to do three things: Confess my mental adultery — because that is what it was — to God and seek for His forgiveness; tell Jeff that we must only meet in the company of other people; let Kate know when we were going to meet so that she could pray for us.

---

*Christians aren't immune to
sexual temptation. And if our partner
is disinterested or even hostile
towards the things we long to share,
it is very easy to become emotionally
involved with someone who
will understand*

I wept many and bitter tears, but somehow I struggled to the end of the project with those promises intact. I shudder to think how close I came to turning my back on all that I knew was right, and breaking up my marriage. Especially as, six months after that, a really dynamic Christian joined Roger's firm, and through his influence Roger very slowly found his way back to God.'

The point of no return

Gina managed to pull back from the brink of ending her marriage, and was very thankful that she had done so. But we have to ask whether a marriage in which at least one of the partners is a committed Christian ever passes the point where the relationship can be salvaged? As we have seen earlier, the New Testament teaches that the fact of one's partner not sharing one's faith is not sufficient reason in itself for the Christian husband or wife to leave. And there have been many

many occasions when God has enabled a fresh start to be made in seemingly hopeless situations. However, when there is physical or mental abuse which simply does not yield to prayer and counselling, or where the abusive partner refuses to acknowledge that there is a problem, there may come a time to say that enough is enough.

Cherry married Don when they were both in their early thirties after a whirlwind courtship. She had been a Christian for a number of years; he professed conversion while they were going out together. Their marriage was extremely difficult, almost from the word go. Don was a very troubled person who had many problems that stemmed from a childhood spent in and out of care. He spent the first ten years of their marriage alternately recommitting his life to God and then denying that he had ever had a faith. He was obsessed with being financially secure, and watched Cherry's spending like a hawk. After their two children were born he insisted that she returned to work as soon as possible, but gave her no say in how her earnings were spent.

Don eventually joined a group of Christians who were extremely legalistic about how life should be lived, and if Cherry or the children displeased him would often go for days without speaking to them. This had its inevitable effect on the children, and after many attempts to get Don to join her in counselling Cherry finally reached the end of her tether.

'Our daughter had just been placed in a unit for disturbed adolescents,' she said, 'and our son was threatening to move into a squat with friends. I had done everything I knew to keep our marriage together, because I thought the children needed the security, but on the day that the social workers took Susie into care, I felt a total failure.

'Later that week I had a slight car accident, and ended up with whiplash injuries. My doctor told me not to go home, but to go and stay with a colleague for two weeks for a total rest. While I was there I realized that having made the break, I didn't have to go back. I longed to be free of all the pain and tension in my marriage, but I also believed that Christians shouldn't divorce. So I prayed, asking God that if it was right for me to leave Don, He would prompt my colleague to suggest an alternative place for me to live, without me saying anything about it. Two days later, completely unprompted, she told me about some flats that were now available for hospital staff at a very modest rent. I took this as God's answer, and told Don that I wouldn't be coming home.'

This happened several years ago and Cherry is now divorced. She says that she still feels guilty at times for initiating the break-up, but on the other hand wonders if she might have saved her children a great deal of emotional damage if she had done it sooner. 'I did what I thought to be right at the time,' she said, 'now all I can do is to leave the final outcome to God.'

15

One Of The Family?

FINDING YOUR PLACE IN THE CHURCH

'When I was a small child,' said Anne, 'I loved books about large happy families like *Little House on the Prairie.* Being an only child with no relations living nearby, I used to think it must be the most marvellous thing in the world to belong to a big supportive clan, who would always be there for you. I didn't know then about family feuds, or that you don't necessarily understand one another, or even like one another very much, just because you're related.'

What picture does the word 'family' conjure up for you? Depending on our experience of our own extended family, our reactions are likely to be very varied. God intended the family unit to be strong and the foundation on which a healthy society would be built. Sin and selfishness has gone a long way to wreck that ideal, and these days we hear a lot about 'dysfunctional' families where relationships don't work well. However that doesn't alter the fact that there is wonderful security in being part of a group of people who do love and support one another. In the New Testament the church was often described as a family. In his letter to the Ephesians Paul wrote:

> So then, you...are not foreigners or strangers any

longer, you are now fellow citizens with God's people and members of the family of God.

Ephesians 2:19

When we become Christians, we aren't intended to feel like strangers from God and His people any longer. No matter what our blood relations are like, we are now part of a brand new family. Most of us experience this by being part of the local church.

Getting to know you

It can come as a bit of a shock to a new Christian to discover that the family of God on earth isn't perfect either! The trouble is that we don't stop being human when we ask Jesus into our life, and the changes that the Holy Spirit brings in our personality develop slowly. Jesus had to demonstrate what loving one another really meant, to disciples who had been in his company for three solid years. Paul had a number of very strong words of correction to say to the first Christians about their attitudes to one another. So I suppose that it's hardly surprising that many Christians who come to church without their partner aren't always as well understood or cared for as they might be.

We have already seen what a struggle many people find it to worship alone, in a partner-oriented atmosphere, week after week. It's very hard to feel torn between loyalty to our partner and children, and the church responsibilities that we would love to take on in order to serve God within the fellowship. Special events that others look forward to can be just another source of friction and isolation if our attendance causes conflict at home. And hardest of all to cope with is the implication, often thoughtlessly made, that if the lone believer were a 'better' Christian or husband/wife, their partner would have come to faith long since.

'I find it so hurtful that couples at church don't seem to be aware of these things,' said Donna sadly. 'I don't want to be pitied or regarded as some sort of freak. But it would be wonderful for my situation to be understood. And if some real attempt was made to recognize and help me deal with the particular problems I face, it would be such an encouragement.'

Communication is the key

It *is* very difficult to truly understand a life situation that we've not personally experienced. And just as in an ordinary family good communication is the key to understanding one another better, so within the church we need to talk and listen to one another. This isn't easy. In years gone by, the stiff upper lip was seen as often inside the church as out of it. People tended to act as though once you'd committed your life to Jesus, you'd had all your needs met and that was that. So anyone who admitted to needing help, was liable to be regarded as a second class Christian.

Thankfully that attitude is gradually dying out. But many of us still find it difficult to confront unhelpful attitudes when we come across them, or be honest about the difficulties we face. However, until we do, nothing is likely to change. So let's see how we can speak the truth in love, within the church family.

The first thing that we can do is to look around the church for others in the same position and we can form what we could call a 'support group'. If, like Clare, you go to a large church, you may have to ask the minister who else is worshipping alone. Clare's minister took the initiative, once he recognized the need, and invited the women whom he knew had not-yet-believing partners to meet at the vicarage. Other women have met in one another's homes, or on church premises. They rarely have their meetings formally announced, because there may be some uncommitted partners who are attending church, and this could cause them hurt or embarrassment.

In years gone by, the stiff upper lip was seen as often inside the church as out of it. People tended to act as though once you'd committed your life to Jesus, you'd had all your needs met and that was that

---

What does a support group do?

The programme that people adopt for their meetings is as varied as the needs of those within the group. Jackie meets with four other women of a similar age to herself, on a weekday morning, once a fortnight in term time. 'We've become really close friends,' she said. 'We see ourselves as a power house of prayer for our husbands and children. We do share our problems and encourage one another, but our primary focus is prayer. In the nine months since we've begun to pray together, we've seen one husband come back to faith, another has started to come to church occasionally and another regularly. We meet each other as couples through school and other local functions, so our husbands do know one another. We've had a couple of social evenings…a barbecue in the summer, and we went to a PTA supper and disco together. In this way we hope that when they come to faith they'll have existing friendships and so be able to support one another.'

Jenny belongs to a group that is rather different. They only meet once a month, have about ten regular attenders of widely different ages, and up to sixteen women on occasions. 'Our meetings are held in the church lounge,' she said, 'because none of us felt comfortable about discussing our problems or praying for our partners in their own homes. We're women from all sorts of backgrounds and at various stages of spiritual experience. One has been a Christian for six months, while another has been praying for her husband to come to faith for thirty-five years. The things we do vary from month to month. Among other things we've had:

- A Bible study on Esther — she was the only believer in her household.
- An evening looking at practical matters like giving, finding opportunities to pray, how to explain what we believe, etc.
- A 'Desert Island books and Bible verses' where we shared information about books and passages from the Bible that had helped us.
- Evenings devoted entirely to prayer
- A Christian counsellor who spoke to us about communication and then led us through some hilarious role plays, to practice our new skills.

Since this group is larger, they have an 'adopt a couple' scheme. The names of the couples represented in the group are put into a hat every six months, and then each of the women pull one out and commit themselves to pray for that couple daily. They also try to travel together to any church function that might entail them being late home. 'We understand how important it is to be back at the time we say we will,' said Pam. 'Couples who are there together, can afford to be relaxed, but it's embarrassing if you're waiting anxiously for a lift and they're enjoying a leisurely chat.'

The pleasures and pitfalls of support groups

All the people I've spoken to, who've been involved in a group specifically for Christians with uncommitted partners have agreed that it has really made a difference to their lives.

'I've lost that sense of isolation,' said Pam. 'We don't fit in with the singles totally but we don't always feel comfortable with family events either. They simply remind us that our families aren't with us. So to have others to do things with, who know the kind of situation I may have left behind at home, and will be praying for me when I go back, is wonderful.'

Other benefits that were mentioned are:

- Realizing that the pressures and temptations that I thought were peculiar to me were actually common to us all.
- Being able to get realistic advice in specific situations.
- Knowing that I'm not alone, but one of a large number entrusted with being God's sole representative at home.
- We've all seen our husbands change — whether in their attitude to the church, or in their behaviour within the marriage.

Good and helpful though a support group can be, there are a few things to beware of. It's not a good idea for this to be our only network of relationships within the church, or it can become inward looking, or turn into a 'pity party'! If time and circumstances can possibly be made to permit, belonging to another small group for Bible study and prayer or taking on responsibility with others in the church is very important. There's nothing like working together to forge strong links of love and concern. And however difficult our situation may be, and however much help we may feel that we need, it's important to be aware of others (whether with a Christian partner or none at all) who would appreciate *our* loving and prayerful care. We all have something to contribute.

Two are better than one

It is very difficult to confront negative or unhelpful attitudes alone when we come across them, and this is where having the support of someone who experiences the same problem can make a real difference. Louise and Sue were very frustrated, because the men in their church arranged social events among themselves, but either didn't include any of the 'fringe' men, or expected their wives to issue the invitation.

'I used to sit there and fume inwardly when the church cricket team had their matches and practices announced,' said Louise. 'And the wives were told to use this as an outreach opportunity and get their husbands to come along. Pete is mad on cricket, and had had no opportunity to play since we moved from a village into the town. But he would never come and play with a bunch of strangers because I suggested it. He's a qualified umpire and kept saying that he'd find a team but never did.'

'One day I felt so angry that I poured it all out to Sue. She persuaded me to tell Neil, who organized the church sports teams, how I was feeling. I wasn't sure that I could do that on my own, so we went and had a chat with him together. I tried not to be too confrontational, but even so Neil was quite defensive.

'I made the point that there were a number of men

in contact with the church because their wives were Christians, who would view an invitation to play sport, from another man, a lot more favourably than being asked to a Bible study or Sunday service by their wives. I didn't say any more — but Sue and I prayed. After a week or two Neil asked if he could pop round and see Pete, as they needed an umpire for the next Saturday. He did it while I was out and to my amazement Peter agreed to help 'just this once'. He did, and it soon became a weekly fixture. He hasn't come to church yet, but he spends time with men who are Christians now, and he's discovered that they're normal human beings.'

We've already seen that men aren't particularly good at forming deep friendships with their own sex, and yet this is one of the most effective ways of men being reached with the Christian faith. It is extremely hard, though, for women to say this in a way that will have a positive effect, as Meg discovered.

'I'd tried to point out the need for men to reach out to other men,' she said, 'and suggested a men's supper in the function room at the local pub. But that went down like a lead balloon! I should have expected it. None of us likes to be told what to do. So when there was an evangelism planning group set up in our church, I gave up other responsibilities in order to join it. This gave me the right opportunity to make suggestions about seeker-friendly services, and social events that would act as a bridge into the church for uncommitted partners. One of the best things we did in terms of making contact with my husband, was to ask him to help to lay on a water sports day for the church at his sailing school. He is used to being in charge, and so he felt comfortable dealing with people from the church in an area where he is an expert.'

Little things mean a lot

A church that was holding a Family Festival took a bold step just recently. Some of the Christians who had uncommitted partners were invited to talk to the rest of the congregation about how they could be cared for more effectively. Gillian was fascinated when she heard about it. 'If I had that opportunity I know what I would want to say,' she said wistfully.

'It's the little things which may seem so unimportant in themselves, which I would like to make people aware of. I long for people at church to know George as a person, and to take an interest in him for himself, and not as a potential "soul" to be won. I wish that those couples who naturally have something in common with us — other business men or those with similar aged children would include us in a group of others for a purely social evening. And, on the odd occasions when George does turn up at church, to make him welcome but not overwhelm him or treat him like a someone from another planet.'

'I wish that they would listen to what I say, and not just automatically slot us into a pigeon hole — "rocky marriage" or "intellectual difficulties" seem to be the favourite ones for us — or give me advice about problems that don't exist while ignoring those that do! It would be so encouraging if someone would tell me how well I'm doing — just occasionally — rather than appearing to criticize me for falling short in areas like giving. Couples who give jointly need to be aware that if I don't have any earned income of my own, I can't give money to God's work as freely as I would like to.'

Money, money, money!

Our church was embarking on a major building project

and the focus of that morning's sermon was the biblical teaching about giving. The Old Testament standard of giving one-tenth of one's income as a tithe was explained, and we were asked to think about whether we were meeting that standard and challenged to give over and above that, for this special need. The retired and those on state benefits were encouraged to give a small amount cheerfully; the couples who were both working were faced with their greater opportunity to be generous. But no reference was made to the dilemma faced by those who had an uncommitted partner, and little or no disposable income of their own.

'It's as if I don't exist,' said Julie sadly. 'Either I feel guilty, or as if my contribution isn't important. But this is my church and I want to be part of what is going on. I just don't know how to do it, without causing trouble at home.'

Sadly this is a common problem. Church leaders don't mean to be insensitive, but they tend to forget that finance is a thorny subject in many relationships and the church is often seen as 'being after your money' by those who don't attend. So if this is a difficult area for us, how can we handle our giving in such a way that God is honoured and our partner is happy?

Compromise and communication

The Bible teaches that all that we have is given to us by God, and so anything we give to Him is simply a token of that. The Jewish Christians in the New Testament would have been brought up with the idea of giving a tenth of their income. Christians who keep to that principle today often tell stories about how God has supplied their needs when they really felt that they couldn't afford to give, but did so anyway. If we have a problem about being free to give, some of these questions might help us to sort out a workable pattern.

• **Do I have any money that I'm able to spend as I choose?** If so what proportion of that does God want me to give? Should it all go directly to my church, or are there missionaries or other Christian work that I want to support?

• **What is my partner's attitude to giving?** If he or she is reluctant to see money given directly to the church, are there good causes which we could both support with enthusiasm?

• **If I have little or no money to give, can I give time or my skills?** Can I make a point of shopping for cards, books and gifts from my local Christian bookshop or a catalogue like Tearcraft or Traidcraft which benefits Christian work in the Third world?

• **Have I ever discussed giving with my partner**, or simply assumed that he or she would be against it? If I haven't, should I prayerfully do so?

Hilary had never bothered to mention the subject to Hugh, because she thought that he would be negative about that as about so many other things in their marriage. She simply gave money out of her housekeeping allowance as she had no personal income. She did this without telling Hugh, and felt very uncomfortable about it. However, when Marie, a Christian counsellor, came to talk to the support group that she attended, she was shown a new skill which made communicating on sensitive issues a great deal easier.

'There are five steps to take,' Marie told them, 'and I use the word LEMON to remind me to cover them all. Imagine that you have a subject that you need to discuss, and so at an appropriate moment, when you've time to talk and aren't tired or preoccupied with other things, you ask your partner "What do you think about...?" Then you "squeeze the lemon"!'

L isten to what he or she has to say without interruption

E mpathize — acknowledge that they have a valid point and that you can see where they're coming from. Don't argue.

M y point of view. Explain simply how you see the situation. Don't get heated. This is simply how you see it.

O utcome that I would like to see — explain what you want.

N egotiate. If he or she has a different solution this is where compromise comes in.

Hilary was delighted to find how well Hugh responded. He was pleased to be asked for his view, and encouraged to talk more than he usually did by Hilary's attentive listening. Hilary had come to the conversation primed with facts and figures about how much a homemaker would cost if employed (Hugh is a personnel manager) but found that she didn't need to quote them. He recognized the value of them both having a small regular sum for personal spending out of his income, and agreed that if Hilary wanted to give some of that away, it was entirely up to her. He, in his turn, would be free to 'waste' his money on computer software without Hilary grumbling.

Acceptance and forgiveness

In our natural family there are three things that need saying often and need saying sincerely, in order to keep the wheel of our life together running smoothly. 'Thank you', 'I'm sorry' and 'I love you' are words that we all need to hear, and what applies to our partners and children is just as relevant to our Christian family. In this chapter, we have looked at some of the difficult aspects of being the lone half of a marriage partnership in a church. But there are many positive things to be thankful for, and we need to acknowledge those too.

Richard had been looking for a way out of his marriage for many years, but was afraid that his leaving could result in Lucy committing suicide, as she had often threatened to do. When Lucy became a Christian, Richard saw how she was loved and cared for by her church, took his opportunity and left home. 'I knew that she would be alright now,' he explained. 'These people really know how to care for their own!'

In one sense that's a very negative outcome, but it does show how unbelievers, standing at a distance, often appreciate what the church family has to offer, more than those of us who are closer to it. So let's be ready to focus on the positive, as well as confronting the negative where necessary. A note of appreciation after a helpful sermon, or a phone call to thank a praying friend for her interest and concern can really lighten someone's day. A willingness to be the one who gives, rather than always to be the focus of care, is good for us as well as the one we help. And above all the ability to see that we could be in the wrong — just sometimes — and be ready to go and apologize and put it right with the person concerned, is truly a sign of the love of Jesus being demonstrated in our lives.

16

Wait For Me

GOD'S TIMING, OUR IMPATIENCE

S omeone once said that God's clocks keep perfect time. This can be very hard to accept when the conversion or return to faith of the one we love so much — the event that we've prayed and longed for most — seems endlessly slow in coming. Sometimes God moves when we have all but given up.

Jane had been a Christian for a number of years, and although her husband was tolerant towards her faith, he showed no sign of wanting to share it with her. One Sunday, after a really stirring service, her friend Irene turned to her sadly. 'Do you think your husband will ever believe and sit here in church with you?' she asked.

'I certainly do,' said Jane. 'God reminded me of a verse in Acts when I was praying for Clive years ago. It says 'Believe in the Lord Jesus and you will be saved — you and your household' (*Acts 16:31*). I really believe that that will happen one day.' Irene shook her head despondently. 'I've given up,' she sighed. 'I don't believe Dick will ever change!'

Two weeks later Irene was confined to bed with a broken leg. It was early in the morning, and as her husband got up, as he usually did, to make a cup of tea, he was overwhelmed with a sense of God's presence and fell to the floor. Irene thought he'd had a heart attack but was unable to get out of bed to do anything to help. Imagine her incredulity and joy when Dick rose to his feet and asked her to pray for him. At that moment he committed himself to God, and from then on was totally changed.

'I couldn't believe it when I heard,' said Jane ruefully. 'If that's what it takes to bring Clive to faith, I'm perfectly willing for God to break my leg, but it hasn't happened yet!'

Beryl's story

God doesn't seem to have any set patterns in the way that He deals with us. Some pray for their partner for a short period before God answers; for others it is a determined pilgrimage of perseverance and prayer. Beryl was one of the latter. She had been sent to Sunday School as a child, but saw no reason not to marry Brian who had many good and upright qualities, but was an agnostic. Seven years after they married she heard Billy Graham preach at Harringay, and committed her life to Jesus.

'I knew I had to tell Brian right away,' she said, 'and it wasn't well received. He said that I would have to do it alone. Initially it wasn't a big divide between us and he would come to Carol and Harvest services with us. My three sons were in the Boys Brigade, and through that organization one of them came to faith, and another became a Christian later.

'I persuaded Brian to take our holiday at Lee Abbey, a Christian Conference Centre. I revelled in the peaceful atmosphere, and hoped and prayed that he would come to trust Jesus then. But he said that he had listened to what the speakers had said, and it definitely wasn't for him. I was sad because I knew increasingly how great it is to be a Christian, and I wanted to share this great joy with him. I couldn't sleep that night and I crept out of bed and stood by the window looking at the moonlit coastline. I made a vow to God that I would pray for Brian always as the most important person in my life. I little dreamed of what that vow would cost me, or where it would take me.'

'Brian became more successful in business and was away far more, often abroad. I got on with running the home and bringing up our family of four. Mostly they were good years and I, at least, was happy. We were, however, heading for rougher waters in our marriage, and just at that point a company move took us north of London. This meant that I had to leave all my Christian friends behind in Kent, but I knew that God had it all in hand.

'As Brian's responsibilities at work increased he became harder and more critical of everything Christian. He wanted to be known as someone who definitely didn't believe, would never believe, and didn't like Christians as a matter of principle! Our son Chris was training for the Anglican ministry by this time, and Brian treated it like a shameful secret. In his view it was a total waste of a good brain and a good degree.

'I came to dread a wet Saturday. In some way, it seemed to be my fault. In my own eyes I was becoming the most inferior person who ever lived. I felt a double failure, that I, as a Christian, couldn't make our marriage happy or even keep it together. One Saturday there was a frantic battle over the bread not being out for breakfast. I see now that Brian was just picking a quarrel to make what he wanted to say easier. He told me that he was going out to Spain to buy a house, taking early retirement and leaving me...and that he would hate me till the day he died. He told me to get a solicitor, as he was going to start divorce proceedings.

It was certainly a black Saturday. I can't remember whether it was raining, but feeling that this was yet another thing that was my fault, I did as I was told, went straight out and got myself a solicitor.

'The period that followed was a living hell. All the outward security of my life had gone. It wasn't a smart time of life to learn how to manage on a limited income. I sometimes wondered whether I was losing my sanity. But throughout all the emotional turmoil I did sense God's nearness. He didn't take sides over the scenes. He was more positive than that. He came alongside me and gave me the grace to forgive Brian and to receive His forgiveness for myself. For although I didn't shout and rage back when Brian berated me and my faith, I certainly needed forgiving for my thoughts.

'It was very difficult to tell my family and friends what had happened. I felt so humiliated that I, as church warden, had a broken marriage. I felt that my witness as a Christian was ruined. One day I had some invitations to give out to neighbours for an outreach event in the town. I stood in the garage with the cards clutched in sweaty palms, and a heart like lead. But God said, "Go! You may be surprised." And I was! Everyone I asked accepted the invitation, and when the day came there was a whole row of people I'd invited listening to the Good News. God guarded my reputation and was still able to use me in His service.

'The day came when Brian was ready to leave. It was strange to see him packing all he wanted to take with him in a left hand drive car. It was stranger still that he bought me a big bunch of carnations, saying that he was sorry that it had worked out this way but he knew he would be happier. I didn't have an answer for that! I'd bought a Bible for him, and somehow had to get it into the car, which was loaded to the brim and locked.

I asked the Lord for ten minutes to do this. Suddenly Brian went out of the front door, moved the car and parked it round the back of the house, leaving it unlocked. I flew out of the back door and slid the Bible onto the floor of the car. It survived the journey to Spain, and was actually put onto the bookshelves in his new home.

'I prayed for his safe travel that night, although I could only do it silently — the stress had completely taken away my voice. And I kept on praying, remembering what Jesus had said in Luke 18 about the unjust judge and the persistent widow. Through that story Jesus assured us that if this hard-hearted judge would listen to this woman, how much more would our God, who has a heart of love, delight to give us the desires of our hearts, and respond to our needs. Sometimes though, we have to trust him where we cannot see, and where there is apparently no hope, persist, and go on praying with the help of the Holy Spirit.

'I have to confess that at times it did seem pointless. He had everything going for him — ample money, a perpetual holiday in Spain and much foreign travel. The devil often used to whisper in my ear, "Give up! He's never going to be saved. Isn't it obvious?" I fought back with God's word. "God wants all men to be saved and come to the knowledge of the truth" (*1 Timothy 2:4*). That is my confidence and seal on praying for such a man. But it was hard, hard work. I found great help and encouragement from reading — books, and particularly the Psalms. In them I found the daily, and sometimes hourly, strength to go on.

'The divorce took forever — three-and-a-half years in all, ending with a three day full court hearing in London over all the finances. I was amazed how God kept me through that time. Before he left I had said to

Brian, "The God whom I serve will not see me brought to ruin and you will see this." It took considerable courage to say it and his response was, "God doesn't exist." So I prayed that God would be glorified through the hearing in London.

'My counsel led me through various areas of my life, and the fact that I was a Christian came out very clearly. I looked at the ten or so people round the table, and no one scoffed or laughed that one should be a Christian and live it out. So Brian had to sit and listen and see that God had kept me and brought me to that point, preserved from a breakdown and still serving Him and caring for the family. In the end, it wasn't a question of money but of God being upheld and glorified, and that is what happened.

> *Sometimes though, we have to*
> *trust Him where we cannot see,*
> *and where there is apparently no hope,*
> *persist, and go on praying with*
> *the help of the Holy Spirit*

'Brian looked unwell at the hearing, and soon after returning to Spain it became obvious that he was really sick. He'd wanted to be on his own and now he was both alone and ill. The Spanish doctor wouldn't even visit him. Our youngest son went out to Spain and brought him back to England. He came through the airport in a wheelchair. Quite incredibly and all in God's plan, he agreed to go and stay with our eldest son Richard, who had, by now, become a Christian, and lived near my old church and Christian friends. They began to pray for him.

'Soon he was diagnosed as having cancer, and he had to have surgery. Sheila, one of my Christian friends from years back went to visit him in hospital. She asked if she could pray for him. Before he could refuse, our daughter Penny, who had just arrived at his bedside, said "Father, you're going to need all the help you can get." I'm sure that no one had ever prayed *with* (rather than for) Brian before, and, as Sheila prayed, she felt such opposition to her words that she said that she nearly fainted. She mentioned terrible pain in her head, and she isn't an hysterical type or given to exaggeration. So the final battle for this man's soul began in the heavenly realms, and although he didn't want me to visit him, I could sense the powers ranged against us all.

'Brian's needs were made a special subject of prayer by the prayer circle at Richard's church, and from home I watched and prayed. It was far from easy at first. It seemed as if I'd just begun to rebuild my life, and now Brian needed to be in the forefront of my thoughts and prayers again. But I found that where human love gives out, as it had, God's totally self-giving love can take over. And that love is a winner, always. I had to be willing to be made available for whatever would be needed and to trust God. I feared being hurt all over again, but this never happened. The healing that I'd received was never, ever in danger.

'Every day the news got worse, and the children needed my love and prayers too. I freed them from coming to see me and we phoned every day. Whenever I went out I seemed to meet people I hadn't seen for ages and told them of the situation. The circle of prayers steadily got larger.

'Brian was now in a nursing home, and a very wise and godly friend went to see him. He talked to Brian very gently about God, and left his Bible there for him to read. The next day it was sent back with a note saying "Thanks, but no thanks." Brian said to someone,

"You know, what I despise most is someone who turns to religion when they're in trouble." The clear implication was "Because I'm dying of cancer I shall not become a Christian."

'When Chris, our minister son, told me that, I couldn't pray for Brian that night. I simply prayed for the children as they drove to their homes. I said to God, "Well that's it, isn't it? He isn't coming to you" and I fell asleep. At 2 a.m. I sat bolt upright in bed and said, "What? Give up now, with just a week or two to go? What's the matter with me, Lord?" So I got up, made myself a cup of tea, and prayed for hours. I was wracked with the urgency of it all. I had a real feeling of panic and a crushing sense that it was all down to me and my prayers. However the next day God showed me a picture of a big circle of people, all with their hands joined, each one in prayer, and me...no more important than the Christian standing either side of me. My whole being was flooded with peace and I never worried or panicked again.

'I sent a card to Brian, something he could look at and find beautiful. He wrote two letters to me, full of gratitude for all that was being done for him, and for the love of the children. He hoped that I was well and enquired about the garden. There was a change of heart very visible in those letters.

'The very next day after I received the second letter, the miracle happened. Brian became a Christian, all on his own in the nursing home. He'd been in great pain for days, and nothing could be done to relieve it. He said to God, "All right God. If this is your way of reaching me, and you will take away my pain, I will turn to you and accept Christ, and there will be no turning back." Instantly there was complete pain relief and peace of heart, which lasted until he died, ten days later.

'He was waiting to tell Chris when he visited him. He didn't say, "I have accepted religion," or even, "I have become a Christian," but "I have come to Jesus." He told everyone who visited him; colleagues from years back, our children and all the staff at the nursing home. He was concerned about our daughter and son who were not yet Christians too.

I found that where human love gives out, as it had, God's totally self-giving love can take over. And that love is a winner, always

---

'What a wonderful answer to thirty-five years of prayer for someone! Christopher, too, had prayed for his father for twenty years, and was praying with him when Brian died. Chris said that he'd never seen such a sovereign act of God in someone's life. One moment Brian was deliberately and determinedly having nothing to do with God, and the next he was soundly converted by the direct intervention of the Spirit of God. Christopher could hardly believe it; I could hardly believe it, but it was wonderfully true. Brian had lost everything that he once counted precious, but he had found the pearl beyond price — life with Jesus for all eternity.

'Chris planned the funeral with his father before he died, and he wanted it stated that he'd come to faith during the last days of his illness. The church was packed with many business people and friends and the effect of the service was amazing. As Brian had been powerful in denying that God existed in his lifetime, so he was powerful from beyond the grave, in telling out the wonderful news of his coming to Christ and the peace that he had found.

'Of course it is sad that we didn't have time to share our faith in our life together, but I've learned to trust God's timing. He sees the whole of time and eternity; the great movements of history and how they fit together, not just our limited viewpoint. Sometimes we know why we had to wait. Sometimes, in this life anyway, we will not know. In the New Testament some of the early Christians thought that God was slow in taking action and the apostle Peter reassures them, "With the Lord, a day is like a thousand years, and a thousand years like a day" (*2 Peter 3:8,9*).

'God has His own perspective. We tend to worry and think that God isn't going to act, or that He's held up. We have doubts that our prayers are heard. We think something has gone wrong. The situation may become so black that we give up. But we must go on asking, trusting, expecting God to act. However long it takes, we must stay faithful and go on...and on...and on...until we see God's answer.

'A song that I used to play over and over again in the dark days by the singer/songwriter Gay Hyde sums it up for me:

> I could never understand
> The pain I had to bear
> Nor why all my dreams
> Could not yet be.
> Till I realised anew
> His presence even there
> And heard him say to me so tenderly
>
> Wait for me
> Wait for My time
> Wait for Me
> Wait for My time
> I know how
> You're feeling now

But trust me still
And wait for My time.

For His Father's perfect timing
Jesus had to wait
My hour's not yet come
He'd often say
Then the same, the cross —
And yet the victory was great
And so with Him I'll walk the perfect way

Still it hasn't been explained
I still don't understand
Why this pain is mine
To bear each day.
Yet it is enough to know
My times are in His hand
He'll hold me up
As these words I obey.

Wait for Me
Wait for My time
Wait for Me
Wait for My time
I know how
You're feeling now
But trust me still
And wait for My time.'

If you want to hear 'Wait for Me' it is to be found on Gay Hyde's tape:
Wait on the Lord. Each tape costs £5. Please send the money with your
order, adding postage, and making cheque payable to E.C.H.O.
Write direct to: ECHO Recordings, 4 Pinery Road, Barnwood, Gloucester,
GL4 7FL.

17

Going Forward Together

THE CHALLENGE OF A SHARED FAITH

'Yes, I'll come to this service of yours, but after tonight I don't want to hear any more about this Christianity business. Enough is enough!'

With these daunting words ringing in her ears, Jenny set off to church for her baptismal service, leaving Paul to follow later. Little did she imagine, that on that very evening Paul would be among those making their way to the front of the church as an indication that he, too, wanted to make a fresh start with Jesus Christ. At that time, Jenny had been a Christian for just about three years.

Beryl and Brian, whose story was told in the previous chapter, didn't have the chance to learn to live out their faith together, but deathbed conversions are rare. For Jenny and Paul, as for many others, his commitment to Jesus meant a whole new way of life for both of them. 'It was a shock,' said Jenny, 'to discover that Paul's new faith meant that I had to change as well. I'd longed for the day when he would believe as I did, but I think that that was the problem. I expected him to be a clone of me in his spiritual life, which was so silly — especially as we're totally different in every other way. I'm thankful that our house group leader pointed out to me pretty early on, that if God had wanted two Jennys

He wouldn't have made one of them Paul! Otherwise I might have trampled Paul's seedling of faith into the ground with my over enthusiasm, and ruined everything.'

Think back to your own beginnings

Jenny's reaction was very natural — we all tend to look at life from our own point of view. And that isn't entirely bad, if it helps us to put ourselves in someone else's shoes. So if you are in the exciting situation of having a new Christian as a marriage partner, think back to how you felt when you started out. Were you a bit bewildered, needing to think things out quietly, uncertain of what to read in the Bible, or how to pray? Did you wonder what on earth you were going to say to your family or friends at work, or were you bursting to tell them? Did you long for someone to explain all those things you couldn't understand, or did you want to take things slowly, and deal with one issue at a time?

This strange new world is where your partner is living now, and in your enthusiasm to share what you have learned beware of swamping him or her with a second-hand faith. Offer advice and help only when it is asked for, and remember that God deals with us all as individuals. So beware of falling into the trap of comparing your partner's experience with your own. *You* wanted to sing worship songs from morning till night when you were a new Christian? Fine! But if your partner doesn't want to, then that's okay too. He or she wants to tell everyone about the wonderful change in their life? Be glad about that, but don't feel guilty because even now you find it difficult to talk to people about your faith. God can meet your needs in that direction just as He will meet your partner's need in another. The important thing is that we each recognize our own needs and bring them to God.

Put the past behind you

If there has been a lot of pain and difficulty in a relationship, it may be tempting to think that once your partner has come to faith, everything will be plain sailing. But that is unrealistic. God does change us, but He does it little by little. And if your partner had a fiery temper, or a tendency to get depressed, that characteristic won't disappear over night. Forgiveness is important too. Adele and Gary had had a lot of problems in their marriage. Gary wasn't good at handling money, got into debt and then started drinking heavily. He lost his job and they ended up being declared bankrupt, losing their home, their car, and most of their possessions. At this rock-bottom point in their lives, Gary finally stopped trying to bail himself out of trouble, and asked God to sort out the mess that he was in.

'At first I just didn't believe it,' said Adele. 'But it wasn't a happy disbelief. It was a wary scepticism, and a fear of being disappointed if this turned out to be as short-lived as some of the other solutions he'd tried. This squashed the joy that I always thought that I'd feel when he finally made a commitment. Bitterness and the habit of blaming your partner can root themselves so deeply that they're incredibly hard to get rid of. You think that you've forgiven for past events, only to find these negative attitudes creeping back at the first sign of difficulty. Money had always been a problem for us, and so all money matters were touchy subjects.

'I finally realized that I could wreck the good things that God was doing in Gary's life, if I didn't deal with this resentfulness. Somebody pointed out a verse in Psalm 37 which was a great help with this. In the New

International Version of verse 8 it says, "Refrain from anger and turn from wrath" which is helpful. But in one of the very old translations it reads, "Let go displeasure" and I had a picture of a game I used to play with the children when they were small. We would drop twigs into the river on one side of the bridge, and then rush across to see whose stick would emerge first. As I thought about that, I had a picture in my mind of me dropping huge branches of anger, fear and bitterness into the swirling river of God's love. Then I stood watching while they were just swept out of sight. Every time the feelings came back I did that in my imagination, and eventually I found that they'd gone for good.

Take a step back

For women like Adele, who had always had to take the major share of responsibility in their relationship, it can be particularly difficult to allow their husband to take a lead in anything, and especially in spiritual matters. But even when this hasn't been the case, many people automatically defer to the wisdom of experience. This isn't always a bad thing, but there are times when it is important to take a step back, and let a baby Christian begin to grow up.

A year or so after Gary became a Christian, both he and Adele felt that God was calling them to move to another church. They were reluctant to leave the familiar where they'd had so much help. 'However much we tried to dismiss it from our minds, it wouldn't go away,' said Adele. 'We prayed and prayed but just couldn't decide what was the right thing to do. Gary kept saying, "I'll go along with whatever you decide" but I couldn't make up my mind. I invited our vicar over to see me, and he wasn't very sympathetic. In fact

I felt really depressed and crushed after two hours of being criticized and questioned.

'Eventually God spoke to me — first through something I read in the Bible, then through a friend who knocked on the door specially to tell me what she felt God was saying, and thirdly through a missionary friend whom I phoned in sheer desperation. In each case the message was essentially the same. 'If you cannot come to a decision jointly, it is your husband's responsibility to decide. Lean on him.'

'I told Gary, and we recognized that we had been handling things in the wrong way. Gary then went to see the vicar, while I prayed fervently that he would really sense what God wanted for us. "I'll go along with whatever he decides, God," I prayed, "but please don't let him come home uncertain still." And he didn't. During the course of a long meeting Gary said that he became more and more convinced that we should move on. I was astonished that someone who was often *so* uncertain about everything could be so certain about this, and felt as if a huge weight had been lifted from my shoulders.'

Take a step forward

One of the joys of sharing your faith with your partner is the opportunity you have to read the Bible and pray things over together. Sadly many couples who have been Christians for years never make this a habit. There are all sorts of reasons for this — lack of time, lack of confidence, and not giving it priority — being three of the major things that Satan uses to distract couples from something that can be a very powerful resource for good in their relationship. But if you possibly can, it's a good thing to make this a habit right from the beginning of your new life together.

As a new Christian, Colin felt self-conscious about praying aloud in case he said something that 'didn't sound right.' Chrissie found herself completely tongue-tied at the thought of praying with the person who knew her best in the world — although she had often prayed with her friends. This situation might have gone on indefinitely, had their minister not visited them at home one evening. He casually suggested that they prayed together before he left and was amused by their horror struck expressions. 'Just a couple of sentences to thank God for what He has done for us will be fine,' he said. 'I'll start, then you Colin, and Chrissie you can round things off for us.' Those prayers were rather faltering and they weren't full of long words and holy language. But they were sincere, the sound barrier was broken, and since then Chrissie and Colin have tried to make a point of praying together every day.

Anne and John pray together less frequently, because John commutes, leaving home early and arriving back late. But on a Sunday evening they compare their diaries for the coming week, and pray about their work and the other things that will fill their time. 'When we tried to pray late at night it didn't work,' said John. 'I was too tired, and often it just seemed like a ritual we were going through. Praying every day may be the ideal, but I feel that it's important to be realistic and do what you can do, rather than giving up because you can't achieve perfection. Praying together this way, we know what the other one expects to face each day, and we can back one another up in our own times of prayer during the week. I think that it has really strengthened our marriage because it makes sure that we stay in touch and honest with each other and with God.'

Throw away your blue-print for a Christian partner

In your day-dreams about that wonderful day when your partner shared your faith, did you build up a glowing picture of exactly how he or she would behave, based on characteristics of the Christian men or women that you admire most?

Did you think that your husband would have the biblical knowledge of David, preach like Tony, be the first to put his hand in his pocket for the needs of others like John, or be a charismatic leader in the church like Peter? Or perhaps, as a man, you imagined a wife who would entertain effortlessly like Helen, wisely and sensitively counsel the hurt and the lonely like Sara or be a gifted and enthusiastic evangelist like Kaye? You did — with a great many other things beside? Then throw away the blueprint quickly before you're tempted to try and force your loved one into a mould, and make one of the biggest mistakes of your life. Praise God for the one He has given you — just as he or she is. In God's own time He may call your partner to preach, teach, counsel or take a leading part in church affairs, but first he or she has to grow as a Christian, and that will happen according to God's pattern, not yours.

People are like plants. They all have their individual growth rates, and no amount of anxious watching over them will make them grow faster than that. Of course you'll want to consider together how you should give to God's work. But give your partner time to learn about the principle of giving to God regularly, before waving a deed of covenant under his nose. Encourage him to take his place in the family of the church, but don't try to rush him into church membership before he is ready, or into church work before he has found his

own feet as a Christian. The story of Philip (in Chapter 14) isn't the only casualty of 'too much too soon' that I've come across.

People are like plants. They all have their individual growth rates, and no amount of anxious watching over them will make them grow faster than that

---

On the other hand, avoid being over-protective, shielding him from the pressures that God intends should help him grow. There is no need to fuss around anxiously like a hen with one chick. 'Oh no, I don't think that you should ask Ben to read the lesson this evening — he's never read the Bible in public before.'

Does that really matter? There's a first time for everyone! Maybe this isn't the time for Ben to make a start, but if we throw away the cotton wool, Ben has a chance to decide for himself whether the Holy Spirit is leading him on to do something new. We can pray about these things together, of course; give advice if it is asked for, and be generous in praise and encouragement as each new step is taken. So let's avoid chivvying, criticizing or cosseting, but pray for one another constantly, confident that God who has answered our prayers and called us both to Himself will lead us on, in the words of Paul:

> To understand what He wants you to do, and make you wise about spiritual things, that the way you live will always please the Lord and honour Him, that you will always be doing good kind things for others, all the time learning to know God better and better...praying too, that you will be filled with His mighty glorious strength, so that you can keep going no matter what happens — always full of the joy of the Lord, and always thankful to the Father, who has made us fit to share in all the wonderful things that belong to those who live in the kingdom of light.
>
> *Colossians 1:9-12*, Living Bible

18

And Finally...

They sat in my lounge drinking coffee — not all young mums this time, but a group of women ranging in age from mid-twenties to early sixties. They came from different backgrounds and churches, but they had one thing in common. They all had first-hand experience of living as a 'lone' Christian within their family circle.

But today was special. Today, Anna was bubbling over with excitement, because after ten long years her husband had committed his life to God at the men's dinner he had attended the week before. We listened sympathetically as she told us how impossible life had seemed for the previous two years. We were encouraged by the fact that she could now see the ways in which God had been at work in both of them, during the weeks and months leading up to that wonderful night. But after the others had left, Mary lingered, and finally burst into tears. 'I wouldn't spoil Anna's day for anything,' she sobbed, 'but why doesn't God do something for me? After eighteen years haven't I waited long enough? Doesn't He hear my prayers — what else do I have to do?'

Perhaps that's how you feel as you reach the end of this book. You've prayed until you have housemaid's knee, and talked about the wonderful things God has done for you until it's become a taboo subject. Or perhaps you've gone the 'win them without a word' route, but now feel that if you had said more, things would be different. Maybe, like Jane in Chapter 16, you've prayed, 'Break my leg Lord, if that's what it takes for my loved one to come to you. I'm willing for anything; just do it — and please make it soon.' And still nothing appears to happen. Where do you go from here?

There is only one person who has the answer — and that is God himself. He knows our pain and our struggles and He says:

> 'Trust Me — I gave my life for you because you are so precious to Me. You trusted Me at the beginning of your spiritual journey, trust Me now. Nothing is beyond my power.
>
> Trust Me — I love you and I love those you love more than you will ever understand. You always have been and always will be my beloved.
>
> Trust Me — I can carry you and yours. I long for you to lean on Me with the utter restfulness and assurance of a sleeping child.
>
> Trust Me — I am your shepherd, and I will lead you in the right paths and see to it that you lack nothing that is good.

And as He asks us to trust Him, so God trusts us. He trusts us to accept the unexplained, and not to turn back. He trusts us not to look back and regret His dealings with us in the past. He trusts us not to question Him constantly about the present or fear for the future. We can be certain, beyond a doubt, that He whom we love and in whom we believed at the beginning is able both to keep us and that precious thing or person that we have committed to Him. So we can relax, and with our hand held firmly in His, we can live one day at a time, experiencing for ourselves the truth of the prophet Isaiah's words when he wrote:

> You, Lord give perfect peace to those who keep their purpose firm and put their trust in you.
>
> *Isaiah 26:3*, GNB

RECOMMENDED READING

If you need help in reading and understanding the Bible there are a number of different Bible Reading schemes which you will find available on your church bookstall, if you have one, or from your local Christian bookshop. There are several versions of the Bible divided up into a portion for each day, so that you can read the whole Bible in a year. Explanatory notes on suggested passages are also available in different styles for adults and children.

Scripture Union, 207–209 Queensway, Bletchley, Bucks. MK2 2EB Tel: 019088-56000 produces:

Alive to God for those who prefer a reflective approach to the Bible. On different days, the notes give ideas for worship, prayer and meditation arising from the Bible passage, and then suggestions for action.

Daily Bread gives a brief overall view of each new part of the Bible, before you begin to read it in detail. It focuses on giving jargon free explanation of the meaning of the text, with helpful charts and diagrams where these are appropriate. The notes also encourage application of the truth of what has been read to our own lives.

Encounter with God is for those who want to think deeply about the Bible message, and are probably most suitable for those who have been a Christian for some time.

CWR, Waverley Abbey House, Waverley Lane, Farnham, Surrey GU9 8EP produces:

Every Day with Jesus. This series of notes often takes the reader through Biblical themes rather than working through individual books of the Bible. There is an *Every Day with Jesus for New Christians*, which is helpful for those exploring the basics of the faith.

The Bible Reading Fellowship, Sandy Lane West, Oxford OX4 5HG produces:

New Daylight covers four months of the year, with the Bible text for each day's reading printed out in full. This is followed with a comment or explanation, and a suggestion for prayer or meditation.

Guidelines also covers four months, but is arranged in weekly units. Each weeks' material is broken up into at least six sections, so that it can be used each day, or read through at one sitting.

Bibliography for *Loving God, But Still Loving You*

Bridger, Francis. *Children Finding Faith*. Scripture Union: London, 1988.

Cook, Derek. *Men: What's missing in Today's Church?* Marshall Pickering: London, 1992.

Davis, Linda. *How to be the Happy wife of an Unsaved Husband*. Whitaker House. Springdale, USA.

Jacobsen, Wayne. *The Vineyard*. Harvest House Publishers: Eugene, USA, 1992.

Nouwen, Henri JM. *Life of the Beloved*. Hodder & Stoughton: London, 1993.